Mining Your Database

Making More Sales
Through People
You Already Know

Mining Your Database

Making More Sales
Through People
You Already Know

Steve Hoffacker

AICP, CAASH, CAPS, CGA, CGP, CMP, CSP, MCSP, MIRM

Mining Your Database

Making More Sales Through People You Already Know

© 2013 by HOFFACKER ASSOCIATES LLC
West Palm Beach, Florida, USA

ISBN: 978-0-615-80468-2

———

To sell what you offer, you can wait for interested people to come to you from various sources of marketing and promotion, or you can go out and attract potential customers yourself. You can take responsibility for producing your own leads by intentionally meeting new people and developing those contacts — or you can generate new business by working with people that you already know and who know you.

———

Other Sales Content
By Steve Hoffacker

To access or learn about books, eBooks, articles, blogs, commentary, and other content by Steve Hoffacker for anyone who sells products or services for a living, use the sites below.

"Hoffacker Associates" Website
http://stevehoffacker.com

"Steve Hoffacker's Sales Training Tips" Blog
http://www.stevehoffacker.com/tips.html

Steve Hoffacker's Amazon.com Author Page
http://amazon.com/author/stevehoffacker

"Steve Hoffacker's Home Sales Insights" Blog
http://homesalesinsights.com

Steve Hoffacker's "Sales Quips" Blog
http://salesquips.com

Steve Hoffacker and Hoffacker Associates can be found online at Facebook, Active Rain, Pinterest, Linked-In, Plaxo, Twitter, Goggle+, YouTube, Tumblr, and other business, real estate, and social sites.

Table Of Contents

Preface

I appreciate that you bought this book and that you are reading it — particularly because of the importance of this subject.

It demonstrates that you are interested in being an even better, stronger, more productive salesperson for your products or services than you are right now.

It also shows me that you are willing to take personal responsibility for generating the leads that it will take to sustain you in business.

Depending on what type of sales you are doing, you may find that your customary traffic and sales activity is slower or harder to identify.

Even in more stable market conditions, you might find that you want more traffic or leads than you typically are getting through conventional or traditional means (print advertising, signage, agents, and your website).

Still, regardless of what type of market conditions you may find yourself in, you can take responsibility for the amount of traffic or leads that you get to work with.

You can impact the amount of business you have.

You literally can take matters into your own hands.

I like to think of the general theme of what I am presenting to you as "generating customers without advertising."

Typically, sales are made by having the customer (the interested party) contact you or visit your showroom or sales center.

Usually they hear about your company or products and services through traditional advertising, such as the newspaper. They may also see your website or notice a billboard or directional sign.

Nevertheless, these are ways of attracting customers to you or your location that your company provides for you or that you do for yourself, but they can only do so much to bring new customers to you.

Sometimes this is sufficient to make the number of sales that you or your company want you to make. Sometimes it isn't.

Even in good markets, you can supplement the amount of traffic you are receiving and the number of sales you are making by using the concepts and techniques in this book.

However, when sales are slow or you are competing with other companies or colleagues for a finite number of new customers, the techniques in this book can make all the difference in how successful you are.

I want you to be a self-generator of traffic.

I don't want you to feel like you have to rely solely on traffic that calls you or walks through your front door that you had no hand in generating.

I don't want you to be dependent just on the traffic or leads that traditional or conventional types of advertising and promotion create for you.

In fact, I want you to act as though the only presentations that you'll get to make with are people produced from your own efforts.

Treat the traffic and leads that traditional, passive marketing produces for you as a bonus.

If you work with other salespeople in your company, this is traffic that you don't have to share or worry about losing to anyone else — because you will have identified and produced it yourself.

I realize that this is probably a major paradigm shift for you, but I want you to act as your entire income is going to come from the people that you produce through your own efforts.

Instead of wondering why you don't have more traffic or

asking your company to spend more money and run more ads, you now can do something about it. You can be in control.

You can do this with no direct cost to your company — or you — other than your typical telephone, email, and postage usage.

This text provides strategies and techniques for generating many potential customers for you and your company by working with people you already know or those that are referred to you by people you know.

There are specific telephone and in-person scenarios as well as email and letter templates that you can use exactly as they are (or close to it), or you can use them as a guide to develop your own style of contact.

It's time to take an active role in generating more traffic and sales, and this text is specifically geared toward helping you develop leads from people that you already know — your existing circle of contacts.

Using Your Network

*Making More Sales
Through People
You Already Know*

1

Why Generate Your Own Leads?

You Don't Control Typical Advertising

If you're like most salespeople, you don't get to control or influence how most of your customers learn about your product or service or how they contact you.

While many people will tell you that they were driving by when they stopped into your sales center or showroom (because that's the easiest response and doesn't require any elaboration), most of your traffic probably visits you because they saw some type of print ad in a newspaper or magazine, noticed a directional sign or billboard, received a direct mail postcard or email, visited your website, saw an online ad, or did an online search.

Perhaps you have radio or television advertising.

Agents or referrals may bring or send interested people as well, and people who have met with you or seen what you have to offer may tell their friends and relatives about you.

Nevertheless, most customers and sales leads typically visit your sales center or showroom through the efforts (and investment) of your company.

Essentially, under this arrangement, there is little direct impact that you can have.

Typical Advertising Is Passive

Regardless of what type of advertising is the most successful for producing leads and ultimately sales for you and your company — or what type you personally favor — the fact is that typical advertising, marketing, and promotion is *passive*.

There is nothing wrong with this or bad about this except that you can't control it, manage it, or count on it — specifically.

You can run ads, broadcast radio and TV spots, send out direct mail, post signs and billboards, and have a website — and it's all passive. The person who has a need for what you're offering has to see the message, identify with it, and then act upon it. That's what makes it *passive*.

There's no way to know how many people or which specific people are going to respond to your message until your front door opens, your telephone rings, or you get an email request for information.

Changing The Formula

The issue with passive traffic — regardless of whether you or your company places the ads or invests in them — is that it's not always as plentiful or consistent as you might like.

The main drawback is that you are not in control.

There's nothing wrong with traffic generated in this manner. In fact, it's an important source of your leads.

Nevertheless, if you did nothing more than just work with the traffic that was generated through conventional or passive advertising and promotion, you would not be able to impact your traffic numbers at all.

You would just have to settle for who showed up and when they arrived — and you'd have to settle for the level of interest and relative ability to make a decision.

However, you can be more in control of the amount — and quality — of the traffic that you receive and get to work with than you are when you just rely on traffic generated through traditional ways.

I'm supposing that newspaper advertising, website visits, or other conventional ways of producing traffic aren't enough for you or that you aren't seeing a sufficient number of people on a consistent basis?

Then, how can you make more traffic materialize?

The answer is by going after it and creating it. Take responsibility for it.

Starting With People Closest To You

Without thinking about it too hard — or getting out a pad and pencil to begin writing down names — there are many people you already know that can begin helping you to grow your business.

The two reasons most of them haven't so far is because you haven't asked for their help and they don't know what you do and that you could use their help.

You may have relatives living near you, and everyone has neighbors — as well as a circle of contacts, friends and other acquaintances.

Depending on where you went to school and how long ago that was, you might also have several former classmates and alumni friends that you see on a regular basis, those that you maintain contact with, and those you see at games and events.

The key in generating leads is tapping into this network of people that you already know to make sure they know what you're doing and that you can use their help.

People Enjoy Helping Each Other

People like to help you when they can. This is a characteristic that all of us have within us.

People enjoy helping each other if they feel that they can and as long as they aren't seriously inconvenienced by doing so.

However, not everyone may be willing or able to help you. That's all right.

Start with the people you know the best and then go from there.

You are looking for are some people that you already know (even ones that you don't know that well or you haven't spoken with in a while) who might have an interest themselves in the products, services, solutions, or opportunities you are offering — or who at least will be able to lead you to other people that they know who may have an interest.

The contacts — through suggestions and introductions — that your friends, relatives, and acquaintances provide for you will include people that you have not met or hadn't thought of who might have an interest in what you offer.

The key to this concept is reaching out to people you already know to let them help you.

There is power in reaching out to people that you already know and in requesting their help to generate new leads.

They want to help, and you certainly can use their help. It's a win-win.

Focusing On People You Know

There are two basic ways to reach out to others for their help in generating leads for your business.

One is by reaching out to strangers — people you haven't met — and I discuss these strategies in a companion book, "**Filling Your Funnel**: *Building Your Business By Reaching Out To Strangers*."

The other is through working with people you already know. That is the subject of this book.

For the examples and strategies in this book, I'm talking about people that you have met or know well enough for them to recognize you or take your call.

You may decide to call upon family, current or former neighbors, business associates, professional contacts, merchants that you patronize, service providers and suppliers that you use, former classmates from high school or college, brokers and other real estate agents, appraisers, home inspectors, home stagers, lenders, mortgage brokers, sorority or fraternity members, military buddies, social acquaintances, members from the church or civic groups that you belong to, people who have purchased products or services from you previously, friends of your spouse or children that you've met, people to whom you have made a presentation who are not interested in what you have to offer, or anyone else that you have met in the past — no matter how long it's been since you've spoken with them.

Time Of Friendship Doesn't Matter

The length of time that you have known someone is not important.

The period of time that has passed since you last spoke with them or saw them in person is not important either.

The fact that you can call someone by name, or text or email them — because you know them well enough to do so and they know you well enough to recognize your name — is more important than how long you've known them, how well you know them, or long it's been since your last contact with them.

You might be life-long friends with someone, or you may only know someone that you met briefly at a social function, seminar, or gathering.

Whether you talk to someone frequently or it was just that one time when you introduced yourselves to each other, people still enjoy helping other people.

People will even help total strangers change a tire, give directions, make up small change at the checkout, phone for assistance, or carry their packages.

If we are willing to do that for people that we don't even know because they need our help and we can supply it, think of how much more people we already know might be willing to help us.

We just need to ask for it.

As long as your request seems reasonable to them, people will generally endeavor to help you if they feel they can.

You're Not Risking Your Friendship

Don't worry about imposing on your friendship or making people uneasy that you've approached them.

You're not going to be asking people to be inconvenienced, embarrassed, or go out-of-their way to help you.

You just want to know if they know anyone — including themselves or their companies — who are looking for a product, service, solution, or opportunity such as you offer.

You're not trying to use your friendship with someone to undermine or exploit it.

You simply want to talk with them about what you offer if it's something appropriate for them or their company — and to tap into their circle of contacts to expand the number of people you can eventually talk with about what you offer.

As long as you do nothing to jeopardize your relationship, you should not be concerned about the simple act of asking people you already know for their help.

You May Not Get Any Help Right Now

They may not be in a position to use what you offer or be able to think of anyone to recommend to you. Still, your friends will have tried to help you.

This is not necessarily a one-time request either.

Someone that you approach now may not be able to use what you are offering or be able to think of anyone to refer to you at that moment. Perhaps what you are selling doesn't match their needs or those of their friends or acquaintances they might refer to you.

However, they might think of someone else or be able to recommend someone the next time you talk with them. Their needs could change as well.

Raising Their Awareness

If you sincerely believe that you represent and offer a good product, service, solution, or opportunity at a reasonable value, you shouldn't hesitate about sharing your story with as many people as possible.

This is why you start with people that you know. You want to help them, and you can use their help.

Approach your friends, relatives, clients, associates, acquaintances, past customers, and others in your circle of contacts. Let them begin thinking of ways that they can help you — directly or with a referral.

If nothing more, you are raising their consciousness and awareness so now they are beginning to think of ways to help you.

It's a fairly reasonable request.

You simply are approaching people that you already know and asking for their help — and it's human nature for people to want to try to help if they can.

Whether you are calling someone, emailing them, texting them, sending them a letter or card, or seeing them in-person, you simply are asking people if they have a need for what you provide (unless you know that they don't) and if they can help you meet someone that you can talk to about what you offer.

There's No Obligation

If one of your friends doesn't want to help you or isn't able to provide any names for you, that's all right. Your friendship or relationship doesn't depend on them being able to help you with a sale or a referral.

Just keep trying with others until you get some help.

You're not trying to create any feeling of guilt or obligation — where they feel they have to look at what you are offering or give you some names or else you will be disappointed in them.

If people that you already know don't have an interest in your product, that's OK. Maybe they'll be able to lead you to someone else who might be.

And on it goes — there's tremendous potential.

The more people you involve in helping you search for potential customers, the more successful you will be at identifying them.

Working For Yourself

Be thankful for the traffic and sales leads that passive marketing provides — through advertising, signage, direct mail, internet, and other sources — but be confident in your own abilities to go beyond that and produce your own leads.

If you work in an office with other people, you won't have to worry about sharing the leads that you generate for yourself — or the commissions from those sales.

Approaching people that you already know about what you offer as well as allowing them to help you locate and identify people to talk with is a great way to supplement the traffic that you get through traditional advertising, signage, and the internet.

You may even get to the point where you will be responsible for the majority of the leads that you get.

In fact, a great attitude or paradigm is to regard the traffic generated by your company as a bonus and to plan on producing all of your own leads yourself.

2

Being A Traffic Generator

Going Past Regular Advertising

I trust that you are not content just to wait for a new customer or lead to find you through the internet, newspaper ads, direct mail, directional signage, or similar resources.

There's nothing wrong with this and it has been the mainstay of traffic production over the years, but it's just not dependable — and it's not sufficient.

While the majority of your business currently may come from these sources, it is not a long-term strategy for success because your competition has essentially the same access to these resources.

You need to be different — in a strategic way.

It takes initiative and innovation to be successful with lead generation.

Go beyond what your competitors are willing to do and take responsibility for producing your own traffic.

How often are there slack periods or lulls in the traffic when you wish that more people were coming in, that they were coming in more consistently, that you could do something about making the telephone ring more often, or that you could set more appointments?

How about having your inbox fill up with qualified email inquiries, or the front door to your showroom or office open more often with people qualified and interested in purchasing what you have to offer?

Don't Just Accept What You Get

You don't have to accept just what comes your way through conventional, passive sources — from ads (print or web), signage, your website, or promotions.

You don't have to work just with the traffic or sales leads that your company provides or produces. You can have considerably more than that and be instrumental in generating it.

You can be a catalyst in generating traffic and filling those void spots when traffic produced through other, more traditional sources is not as strong or consistent as you would like.

Taking Responsibility For More Traffic

Take it upon yourself to go outside the boundaries of your office, sales center, warehouse, or showroom to meet and talk to people you already know who might have a need for what you offer — or can lead you to other people or businesses that you can serve.

This is proactive, intentional contact, and it so often is the missing ingredient in being a totally productive salesperson.

These are advanced lead generation techniques, but anyone can use them.

In the pages of this book that you are now reading are powerful strategies and scenarios for increasing your customer base — all through reaching out to people you already know.

Not everyone who should know about your products, services, solutions, or opportunities may find out about you or what you offer through traditional means.

However, when you actively take your message outside the office, you can identify and approach additional people.

Rather than relying on the traffic that is produced though the efforts of your company or conventional marketing, you now can have a very real stake in the amount of people you get to talk with about what you provide — in their office or location or at your site.

In fact, I have known salespeople who have created such a network of their own leads and a referral base that goes along with it that they actually have decided not to take any new traffic that they didn't generate.

You are capable of creating and producing a substantial portion of your traffic — even as much as all of it — through referrals and proactive self-generation of leads.

Not A Mandatory Action

No one is forcing you to produce your own sales leads, but I imagine that this is important to you since you are reading this book.

Just think of the advantage that you'll have over other salespeople in your marketplace when you become responsible for producing your own leads rather than just relying on customers produced through conventional forms of marketing and traffic generation.

Think of the savings you can achieve for you and your company by not running as many ads or using other forms of passive marketing and promotion because you will be a responsible, effective producer of traffic and sales leads on your own.

Is Self-Generation For You?

Before you get started on your program of generating your own leads to supplement or even replace the traffic that currently is being provided for you, it's important to make the commitment to yourself that this is something that you want to do.

Don't undertake it lightly. It requires time, effort, dedication, and persistence to conduct it properly.

If you already are making so many presentations that you really couldn't comfortably meet another customer during your workday, you may not need to generate any more customers on your own — especially if your sales output is at an acceptable level.

However, conditions are subject to change, and in the future you may find that your traffic is less abundant than it is at present.

This is the power you now have available to you. You can create as many leads as you desire.

Become a traffic generator so that you can have an intentional say in how many leads you have to work with.

Traffic Generation Is Empowering

Knowing that you have the ability to generate your own traffic to supplement what you get — or fail to get — through more traditional means should be very empowering to you.

It can propel you into success while others in your marketplace are struggling or working with the traffic that they customarily get.

Being a traffic-generator means that you never have to be totally dependent upon your company's advertising or marketing for bringing in enough traffic or sales leads for you to be successful.

It means that people that you already know — or their friends and relatives that you can meet — can help you build your business.

This creates a predisposition for liking what you offer before you ever begin your presentation, and they are going to like you and enjoy what you have to say because they are friends of yours — or friends of friends. This is true even if they decide not to purchase.

You have the power to generate your own leads, and this will shape the future of your business.

3

Getting Started

Making The Commitment

The first step in creating additional traffic for yourself is actually making the commitment to begin doing something about the amount and quality of leads that you get.

It's strictly a voluntary program. However, it's willful, intentional, and proactive. It's up to you — and only you — to implement and execute.

It's making the definite decision that you want to go beyond what is produced for you through traditional or conventional advertising, promotions, signage, web pages, agents, and casual referrals (those people that will come in because a friend told them about you).

Once you make the commitment, you can go about accomplishing it. You can formulate a plan. You can have a strategy.

You have so many resources available to you, and working with people you already know is a great way to build your customer base.

Beginning At The Beginning

The easiest and quickest place to start building leads for yourself is with people you already know — regardless of how well you know them or for how long.

It doesn't even matter how long it's been since you last talked with them.

Begin with the most obvious ones: family, friends, neighbors, acquaintances, and existing customers from sales you've already made.

Then you can progress past that to local professionals, businesspeople, places where you typically shop for goods and services, and friends or acquaintances of those friends.

Don't forget to involve your business contacts and acquaintances from church, chambers of commerce, boards of Realtors®, homebuilders associations, Rotary and other civic clubs, condominium or homeowners association (or the association at your office building), or other organizations where you might be a member.

Think beyond the obvious.

Spreading The Word

Don't make any assumptions about your relatives, friends, and acquaintances knowing what you do.

Have you told all of them what you're doing?

Do they realize what you sell?

Are they aware of the opportunities that you have? Are you sure?

Are they a candidate for what you offer? Are they willing to lead you to others?

It's time to find out how much they know about what you're doing, their interest level (if any), and how willing they are to help you identify others that you can meet to discuss what you offer.

Who Do They Know?

When you begin reaching out to your friends, relatives, acquaintances, and circle of contacts with a phone call, email, text message, or personal visit, you initially want to make sure they are aware of what you are doing in case they have a need for what you are offering. You certainly would love to have them purchase from you and have them as a customer as well as a friend.

However, you're just as interested — or even more interested — in who they know that they might be able to introduce to you.

Just keep in mind that it is not necessary that you know someone quite well in order to begin a conversation with them about what you do and what you are offering.

Just Making The Contact

You can approach your circle of friends because they know you.

Then you can determine if there is any interest in what you are offering and take it from there. You may have a potential sale, you may have someone who can give you a referral (or more than one), or you have someone who is polite but disinterested in helping you.

Whatever the outcome, you'll be on your way to generating your own leads and sales.

Beginning with your friends rather than with strangers cuts down on the time needed to sell you and your opportunity. You have a believability and likeability factor already built in.

Also, this is not a cold call so you don't need to create a special reason they should talk to you.

Ways To Make The Contacts

In this book, I provide formats, scripts, and scenarios to use in approaching or re-establishing contact with people you already know — through in-person face-to-face meetings, telephone conversations, and written contact (text, email, instant messaging, or regular mail).

You can use them as they are word-for-word, or you can adapt them to your own personal style.

The opportunities for proactive, intentional contact and renewing of acquaintances are extensive.

Think creatively for places and opportunities to contact or reconnect with people that you know and take your message to them.

Again, look beyond the obvious.

Sometimes you'll want to send an old friend an email or note. Possibly a holiday greeting card. Maybe a text message would even work.

Other times you might just want to drop in on someone or invite them to coffee or lunch.

Phone calls are quite versatile and work well when there's a good chance of actually connecting with the people you are trying to call rather than getting their voice mail or going through a receptionist or an assistant. Cellphones are a good place to start rather than the office phone because this is a more personal form of contact and often connects directly to your friend.

The point is, there are many ways to contact your family, friends, and acquaintances, and you can intersperse the methods and mix them up.

However, I would only use texting or instant messaging to set up a time to talk, to arrange or confirm an appointment for coffee, or as a reminder or follow-up to an earlier conversation.

You are interested in more than just spreading your message. You also want to interact and get some help.

Working Just With People You Know

There are many opportunities for you to meet, contact, and reach out to people that you don't already know or have a relationship with — those you are approaching or meeting for the first time.

I discuss those scenarios and the many opportunities for your success in developing those relationships in my companion book "**Filling Your Funnel**: *Building Your Business By Reaching Out To Strangers*."

This is a valuable part of generating leads for your business.

However, in the book you have in your hands now, I am strictly talking about contacting and working with people that you already know or have at least met briefly at a business or social event — anyone that you know well enough to pick up the phone and call and have them recognize your name and take your call.

Begin with your family and closest circle of friends.

It's important that you let them know what you are doing and that you would like to have their help in identifying potential purchasers for your product.

After all, you would do the same for them if they asked for your help and you knew of some way to help them such as listening to a brief presentation or referring them to someone more interested than you in using what they offered.

People Want To Help You

Whether this is a close family member, a distant relative, someone from the club or organization you belong to, someone from your former or current neighborhood, someone you went to school with, a friend or co-worker of your spouse, someone from activities or sports that you do with your kids, someone whose store you shop at, someone you met only long enough to exchange business cards, or anyone else that you know, the point is that you know — or at least have met — each other.

More than that, you know each other well enough for you to walk into their office, pick up the phone and call them, or send them a note or email and have them talk with you.

You know them well enough to be able to ask for their help and not feel awkward about the request.

Remember that people like to help other people when they can — especially people they know. You just might have to reassure or encourage them that they have a way to help you.

Don't feel that you need to know someone for a certain period of time before you talk about your business — or that people will think less of you because you want to talk business rather than engage in small talk.

Telling Your Story

To begin generating your own leads, you just need to tell your story to more people than typically walk through your front door or contact you through traditional ways such as calling you on the phone for information or sending you an email request.

That's why you'll want to begin with your network of friends, relatives, neighbors, acquaintances, shop owners and managers that you know from trading at their businesses, professionals whose services you use, friends or co-workers of your spouse, coaches and teachers of your kids, and anyone else that you know.

You will begin by making sure they are aware of what you are doing — which company you are working for or if you are in business for yourself, and what product, services, opportunities, or possible solutions you offer.

Let them know your intended audience and who your ideal referral is — even if it's them.

At the same time as you are telling your story and catching up on details in their lives that they want to share with you, you can begin determining if they or their company might have some interest in what you offer (if it appears to be an appropriate product, service, or opportunity for them).

Expanding Your Network

In addition to talking to people you know and making them aware of what you are doing currently, you also want to find out about and meet people that are in their network that you don't already know. This way your database will expand with more people friendly to you and favorable to talking with you.

Ask for an introduction to their friends and acquaintances.

By contacting people you already know and then meeting or learning about people that they know who are unknown or unfamiliar to you, you then can start generating your own traffic and begin ending the total reliance you currently have on the traffic that your company or conventional marketing provides or produces.

It diminishes the dependence on passive marketing and puts you in control.

Four Possible Outcomes

Whether you are meeting and talking with strangers (not the subject of this book but a very important part of your overall lead generation strategy) or interacting with people that you already know — or those you will meet or be introduced to through people you already know — not everyone will have an immediate need for your services.

Some might right now, and some may eventually, but that's only part of the total picture.

When you approach your friends and people you already know and ask for their help, there are four possible outcomes — four things that can result.

First, they can refuse to help you. Don't let this stop you from talking with them. It's a possibility, but only one of four.

Maybe they think they can't help you and don't want to get involved. Maybe they just don't want to help even though they know you and could do so. That's unfortunate, but shake it off and move on.

Second, they can have an immediate need to use whatever it is that you offer or provide, and you can engage and work directly with them.

This means that some of your friends and acquaintances will become your customers themselves.

Third, they may not have an immediate need for what you provide but they likely will or could in the future — and they will share this information with you.

So, you have some friends and acquaintances who will or possibly will become your future customers.

Fourth, they can introduce you or lead you to other people that they know whom they feel might have an interest in talking and working with you — with either an immediate or future need.

This is the power of reaching out to get help from the network of people you know.

Time To Get Started

Now, with all of this background on how you want to work with your friends, relatives, acquaintances, and others that you know to help you generate new leads that you can talk with about your product, service, solution, or opportunity, it's time to actually get started.

That begins on the next page where I present three consecutive chapters of scenarios for you to use in contacting people in-person, by telephone, and in writing (including electronic).

You won't use every approach with each person. Some you may only visit in person. Some you may only call. Some you will more than one approach.

Nevertheless, use these techniques as a starting point and add ones of your own that you like. Feel free to use your own words and style, but this will get you started.

4

Generating Leads In-Person

Opportunities To Interact With People

There are people around you constantly.

You shop, bike, jog, work-out at the club, run errands, pick up the kids or attend events with them (if you have kids), buy gas, eat lunch, get a coffee, go to the grocery store, get your car serviced, go to the doctor or dentist, talk with your attorney, drop off and pick up your clothes at the cleaners, live in your neighborhood, get your mail and packages, worship, eat dinner out, go places on your day off, go places with your spouse (if you're married), play golf, go to the pool or beach, attend committee meetings, volunteer, and probably much more than this in a week's time.

The point is that people are around you all the time.

It's learning to take advantage of these opportunities when you're around others to develop relationships and get their help in growing your business through the obvious networking possibilities that exist.

In some of your travels, you're going to see people that you already know or who are familiar to you by sight — even if you've never exchanged more than a glance, smile, wave, or "hello."

Sometimes you'll see complete strangers. You may or may not even have eye contact with them.

While this chapter focuses on connecting with people you already know or are familiar with, you will be making introductions to total strangers as well.

These former strangers then become people that you have at least met once — no matter how briefly — and then you can employ some of the contact strategies that I talk about in this book.

Making The Connection

In the next two chapters, I discuss ways for you to use telephone and written communication to reach out, contact, and connect with your network of people you already know and raise their awareness level so they will be in a position to work with you or refer others to you from their circle of contacts.

However, before we get to that, this chapter provides ways just to develop an in-person conversation to generate additional leads for yourself.

Use the scenarios (or ones like them) that I present in this chapter and the next two as a guide to developing relationships and referrals.

The suggested scripts in this chapter will help you as you contact people that you do business with, people you have met socially or at business functions, people that you see occasionally, family members, friends that you see often or rarely, people you have sold products or services to or talked with during a presentation, or others that you will have an opportunity to talk with face-to-face about what you are doing, how what you offer can help them, and how you can use their help.

Adapting To Your Own Style

You'll discover from reviewing the scenarios and scripts that follow that there are many ways of saying the same thing — depending on your personal style and the degree of formality that might be called for at the time.

You can say *"I wanted to make sure you knew,"* or *"I'm not sure you are aware"* — or you can express a similar meaning by saying that *"I'm not sure if I ever mentioned,"* *"I don't know if I ever mentioned,"* *"In case*

I never mentioned," "*In case you didn't know,*" or "*I don't think I ever told you.*"

Of course, you'll know the gender of your friends, but I have used the pronouns "*he,*" "*his*" or "*him*" for convenience and to avoid using "*he/she/they*" or "*his/her/their*" or "*him/her/them.*" Obviously, you would use the correct pronouns for the actual situation.

The same is true for people that you would like to have referred to you. They might be a single person or a couple, married or not. In many cases, I have just used the collective pronouns "*they,*" "*their,*" or "*them.*"

In actual usage, substitute the correct pronouns for the situation.

Visit To Businesses You Patronize

Use this scenario to talk with the owner, manager, proprietor, clerk, or employee you see frequently at a business you visit regularly. Even if you haven't talked much to this person other than exchanging smiles or nods, a friendly "hello," or some small talk, you know each other from your regular association. This would apply to such establishments as a bakery, donut or bagel shop, coffee shop, fast food restaurant, food catering trucks, hotel, gas station, convenience store, home improvement or décor center, gift shop, florist, furniture and accessories store, pharmacy, grocery, entertainment center, arcade, auto dealership, tire shop, boutique, equipment rental, hair salon, quick printer, car wash, bicycle shop, fitness center, auto detailer, post office or postal service store, marina, dry cleaner, tailor, or other businesses in your market that you visit on a regular basis. You want to make sure they are aware of what you do, discuss how they can help you, learn if they or their company might have some interest in what you offer (if it is appropriate for them), and determine who they know that might have an interest in what you offer — although not necessarily all in one conversation. You'd also like to display your business cards or flyers for their patrons.

———

"Hi <use their first name>."

[When you greet them, conduct your regular business, normal interaction, and small talk first. Then begin the following discussion about how you'd like their help.]

"Do you have a minute (Am I interrupting anything, Is this a convenient time)?"

NOW IS NOT A GOOD TIME — [You actually speak to your friend, owner, manager, or proprietor, but they are unable to devote any additional time to you now.]

"I'm sorry I caught you at an inconvenient (busy) time."

"*Have I ever mentioned to you (Do you remember that I said, I'm not sure I ever mentioned) that I represent <name of your company or that you have your own business> at <provide the actual location, address, or general description of the area — whatever would make the most sense to your friend>?*"

"*Well, I'd like your help on something.*"

"*I'll stop back by when you have a couple of minutes (when you have time to talk). When would it be convenient for me to come back?*"

[Don't get into a discussion now of what you're looking for — it will keep until your next visit.]

[Wait for response. Agree on a day and time for the return visit if other than your next regular visit to their establishment.]

"*Would you like for me to come here, or would you let me buy you a cup of coffee?*" [Wait for response about location of meeting — their business or store, or a coffee shop they suggest. Then confirm the location, day, and time.]

"*Great. I'll see you <specify the day> at <location>. Thanks.*"

Is Available Now — [The person you want to speak to has

---

time to talk now.] *"Great. I'll make this quick."*

"Have I ever mentioned to you (Do you remember that I said) that I represent <name of your company> (that I have my own business> at <provide the actual location, address, or general description of the area — whatever would make the most sense to your friend>?"

"Well, I'd like your help."

"As you know, I've been trading (shopping, eating, drinking coffee) here for <approximate length of time such as a couple of years, 10 years, etc.>, and I thought maybe you could help me."

[Ask them if they have ever heard of your company, product, or service, or if they had ever considered purchasing or doing what your product, service, solution, or opportunity provides. It doesn't matter if they have.]

[Be careful not to share too much information about your opportunity. You are not trying to deliver a "mini-presentation" even though it might be tempting to do so. You just want to provide a basic description of what you offer so that you establish a frame of reference.]

"I thought that you personally might have some interest or possibly you might know or have heard of someone (two or three people) that might be in the

market for what we (I) provide and that you or they should take a look at (hear about) what we have to offer." [Wait for response.]

[If he or she indicates any kind of interest — for them individually or for their business, depending on what you offer — arrange another time to meet and discuss it in more detail.]

[If he or she volunteers a name or two, write it down and ask for a way to contact that person or persons. Be sure to note the correct spelling and pronunciation. Get first names so you don't sound like a telemarketer or solicitor when you call them, and get permission to use your friend's name when you contact the other people.]

They Have Names to Give You — *"That's great. I will call them and introduce myself and discuss what we offer (what we have to offer) and see what their level of interest might be. Then I'll take it from there."*

"I will call you (drop back in) after I have spoken with them to let you know what happened (how it went)."

"Can you think of anyone else?" [Wait for response.]

"Thanks for your help. See you next time. Good-bye."

No Names to Give You at This Time — *"That's quite all right."*

"I'd like to send you our newsletter (updates, specials) on a periodic basis just so you will be aware of what we're offering."

"Is email OK, or should I just drop it off when I come in?" [Wait for the response. Confirm their email address or determine which one to use. You can also send them your contact information or vCard, and send them a link to your website and blog, if you have one.]

"Fine. If anyone does come to mind that you think should know about what we offer, let me know and we'll take it from there."

"In fact, let me give you some of my business cards so you'll have them available if you're talking to anyone that you think I should meet."

"If you can, let me know who was interested enough to take my card or who you gave one to."

"Would it be OK if I left some of my business cards on your counter or if I came back with a small display?" [Wait for response, and accept the answer either way.]

"You know, I'd love to talk with you some more about what we offer just so you'll have a better idea of it. If you have some interest at that point, fine, but we'll just see how it goes. I'd just like for you to have a better idea of what we're all about when you talk to

*people you know or think of who might be looking for
what we offer."*

[Wait for the response. Either a "yes" or "no" is OK. It
won't affect anything else you've discussed or the help
you're looking for. It may not be convenient for him or
her to meet with you or they may feel that the
appointment was what you wanted all along. If they are
agreeable, however, set the appointment while you're
there.]

*"Thanks for your help. See you again next time (or
specific date of appointment if one is set). Good-bye."*

Visit To Professionals You Patronize

Use this scenario to visit or talk with the owner,
manager, principal, or partner of a professional
services firm that you use on a regular basis — either
personally or through your business. This would apply
to such services as a doctor, dentist, attorney, tax
preparer, accountant, ad agency, architect, consultant,
appraiser, media people, webmaster, land planner, or
others in your market that you or your company maintain a
professional relationship with. You want to make sure they
are aware of what you do, learn if they might have a need
for what you provide, discuss how they can help you,
determine who they know that has an interest in what you
offer — and you'd like to display your business cards or
flyers for their patrons in their shop or possibly advertise

on their website.

———

"*Hi <use their first name>.*" [The person you are asking for might greet you, or there might be a receptionist or assistant. Ask for the person you came to see. If they aren't there or available, decide to wait if it will only be a few minutes, or politely say good-bye and return at another time. You don't need to set an appointment or leave any information. Make sure they know you're a friend or client.]

[When you greet them, conduct your regular business, normal interaction, and small talk first. Then begin the following discussion.] "*Do you have a minute (Is this a convenient time)?*"

NOW IS NOT A GOOD TIME — [You actually speak to the person you are calling on, but they are unable to devote any additional time to you now.] "*I'm sorry I caught you at an inconvenient (busy) time. I realize that I just dropped in without an appointment.*"

"*I'll make this quick. Have I ever mentioned to you (Do you remember that I said) that I represent <name of your company> (I have my own business) at <provide the actual location, address, or general description of the area — whatever would make the most sense to them>?*" [Wait for response, but it doesn't matter whether they remember or not.]

"Well, I'd like your help on something. I'll stop back by when you have a couple of minutes (when you have time to talk). When would it be convenient for me to come back?"

[Don't get into a discussion now of what you're looking for — it will keep until your next visit. Wait for response. Agree on a day and time for the return visit if other than your next regular visit to their establishment.]

"Would you like for me to come here, or would you let me buy you a cup of coffee?" [Wait for response about location of meeting — their business or store or a coffee shop they suggest. Then confirm the location, day, and time.] *"Great. I'll see you <specify the day> at <location>. Thanks."*

Is Available Now — [The person you came to see has time to talk with you now.] *"Great. I'll make this quick."*

"Have I ever mentioned to you (Do you remember that I said) that I represent <name of your company> (I have my own business) at <provide the actual location, address, or general description of the area — whatever would make the most sense to your friend>?"

"Well, I'd like your help. I've been coming here (using your services) for <approximate length of time such as

a couple of years, 10 years, etc. >, and I thought maybe you could help me."

[Ask them if they have ever heard of your company or product or service, but it doesn't matter if they have. Be careful not to share too much information about your opportunity. You are not trying to deliver a "mini-presentation" even though it might be tempting to do so. You just want to provide a basic description of what you offer so that you establish a frame of reference.]

"This is where I need your help."

"I thought that you personally might or possibly you might know or have heard of someone (two or three people) that might be in the market for what we (I) provide and that you or they should take a look at (hear about) what we have to offer." [Wait for response.]

[If he or she indicates any kind of interest — for them individually or for their business, depending on what you offer — arrange another time to meet and discuss it in more detail.]

[If he or she volunteers a name or two, write it down and ask for a way to contact that person or persons. Be sure to note the correct spelling and pronunciation. Get first names so you don't sound like a telemarketer or solicitor when you call them, and get permission to use your friend's name when you contact the other people.]

They Have Names to Give You — *"That's great. I will call them and discuss what we have available and determine if they have any interest in learning more about what we can do. Then, I will call you (drop back by) after I have spoken with them to let you know what happened."*

"Can you think of anyone else?" [Wait for response.] *"Thanks for your help. See you next time. Good-bye."*

No Names to Give You at This Time — *"That's quite all right."*

"I'd like to send you our newsletter (updates, specials) on a periodic basis just so you will be aware of what we're offering. Is email OK, or should I just drop it off when I come in?"

[Wait for the response. Confirm their email address or determine which one to use. You can also send them your contact information or vCard and send them a link to your website and blog, if you have one.]

"Fine. If anyone does come to mind that you think should know about what we offer, let me know and we'll (I'll) take it from there."

"In fact, let me give you some of my business cards so you'll have them available if you're talking to anyone that you think I should meet."

"If you can, let me know who was interested enough to take my card or who you gave one to."

"Would it be OK if I left some of my business cards on your counter or if I came back with a small display?" [Wait for response, and accept the answer either way.]

"You know, I'd love to talk with you some more about what we offer just so you'll have a better idea of it. If you have some interest at that point, fine, but we'll just see how it goes. I'd just like for you to have a better idea of what we're all about when you talk to people you know or think of who might be looking for what we offer."

[Wait for the response. Either a "yes" or "no" is OK. It won't affect anything else you've discussed or the help you're looking for. It may not be convenient for him or her to meet with you or they may feel that the appointment was what you wanted all along. If they are agreeable, however, set the appointment while you're there.]

"Thanks for your help. See you again next time (or specific date of appointment if one is set). Good-bye."

Visit To Banks And Lenders

Use this scenario to talk to the manager, loan officer, or employee of a bank or lending institution that you use for your personal banking, where you have your home mortgage or other consumer loans, and/or where your company has loans or a preferred lending relationship. You want to make sure they are aware of what you do, discuss how they can help you, determine who they know that has an interest in improving their business, office, or home in some way (depending on what you offer). Also, you'd like to display your business cards or flyers for their patrons.

_____

"Hi <use their first name>."

[If the person you came to see is not visible to you, ask for them. If they aren't there or available, you can choose to wait a few minutes or politely say good-bye and return at another time. You don't need to set an appointment or leave any information.]

[When you greet them, conduct your regular business, normal interaction, and small talk first. Then begin the following discussion.]

"Do you have a minute (Is this a convenient time)?"

NOW IS NOT A GOOD TIME — [You actually speak to the person you came to see, but they are unable to devote any additional time to you now.] *"I'm sorry I caught you at an inconvenient (busy) time. I know you're busy so I'll be very brief."*

"Have I ever mentioned to you (Do you remember that I said) that I represent <name of your company> (I have my own business) at <provide the actual location, address, or general description of the area — whatever would make the most sense to them>?" [It doesn't really matter how they answer this. Just continue.]

"Well, I'd like your help on something. I'll stop back by when you have a couple of minutes (when you have time to talk)."

"When would it be convenient for me to come back?" [Don't get into a discussion now of what you're looking for — it will keep until your next visit.]

[Wait for response. Agree on a day and time for the return visit if other than your next regular visit to their facility.]

"Would you like for me to come here, or would you let me buy you a cup of coffee?" [Wait for response about location of meeting — their business or a coffee shop they suggest. Then confirm the location, day, and time.]

"Great. I'll see you <specify the day> at <location>. Thanks."

Is Available Now — [The person you came to see has time to talk with you now.] *"Great. I'll make this quick."*

"Have I ever mentioned to you (Do you remember that I said) that I represent <name of your company> (I have my own business) at <provide the actual location, address, or general description of the area — whatever would make the most sense to your friend>?" [It doesn't really matter how they answer this. Just continue.]

"Well, I'd like your help." [Ask them if they have ever heard of your company or product or service, but it doesn't matter if they have. Just continue with your conversation.]

[Be careful not to share too much information about your opportunity. You are not trying to deliver a "mini-presentation" even though it might be tempting to do so. You just want to provide a basic description of what you offer so that you establish a frame of reference.]

"I thought that you personally might or possibly you might know or have heard of someone (two or three people) that might be in the market for what we (I) provide and that you or they should take a look at (hear about) what we have to offer." [Wait for response.]

[If he or she indicates any kind of interest — for them individually or for their business, depending on what you offer — arrange another time to meet and discuss it in more detail.]

[If he or she volunteers a name or two, write it down and ask for a way to contact that person or persons. Be sure to note the correct spelling and pronunciation. Get first names so you don't sound like a telemarketer or solicitor when you call them, and get permission to use your friend's name when you contact the other people.]

"*Can you think of anyone else?*" [Wait for response.] "*Thanks for your help. See you next time. Good-bye.*"

No Names to Give You at This Time — "*That's quite all right. I'd like to send you our newsletter (updates, specials) on a periodic basis just so you will be aware of what we're offering. Is email OK, or should I just drop it off when I come in?*"

[Wait for the response. Confirm their email address or determine which one to use. You can also send them your contact information or vCard and send them a link to your website and blog, if you have one.]

"*Fine. If anyone does come to mind that you think should know about what we offer, let me know and we'll (I'll) take it from there.*"

"*In fact, let me give you some of my business cards so you'll have them available if you're talking to anyone that you think I should meet. If you can, let me know who was interested enough to take my card or who you gave one to.*"

"*Would you have a place where I could leave some of*

my business cards or put out a small display?" [Wait for response, and accept the answer either way.]

"Thanks for your help. See you again next time. Goodbye."

"Working The Room" With People You Know At A Business Or Social Event

Use this scenario to talk with people you already know at a social event or business function. This can include parties, receptions, mixers, get-togethers, reunions, classes, barbeques, fundraisers, seminars, conventions, trade shows, potluck dinners, ice cream socials, trade association functions, and similar meetings and events. After the small talk, explore their interest level in what you offer (if your product or service is appropriate for them or their business and if you haven't already done so on a previous occasion), and seek their help in identifying people who might have an interest in what you offer (even if you have done this previously — you might have to remind them of what you do or what your ideal referral is). You would like for them to provide an introduction for anyone in the room or event that they feel you should meet. Otherwise, this is a prelude to a longer conversation or meeting outside of the event.

———

"Hi, <first name of your friend>."

[After you exchange greetings and catch up on what each other has been doing, trade business cards if you don't have current contact information for each other. Give yours out anyway. Talk briefly about what you offer. Then, change gears and use the conversation to talk about what you want.]

"I'm working with <name of your company> (I have my own business) — and we're located at <a general description is probably enough>."

"You know, I could really use your help. I thought maybe you could identify some people — possibly even yourself (again only if what you offer is appropriate for them or their company) or some of the people who are here — who might be interested in looking at or considering <general description of your product, service, solution, or opportunity> —- now or in the near future. Possibly some people that you know that I don't."

"Anyone come to mind right now that you have seen here that you think I should meet?" [Wait for response.]

[If yes, ask your friend to introduce you to them. If not, go to the next question.] *"Who (Who else) can you think of that might take my call to let them know about what we offer (provide)?"* [Wait for response.]

[If they volunteer a name or two, write it down and ask for

a way to contact that person or persons. Be sure to note the correct spelling and pronunciation. Get first names so you don't sound like a telemarketer or solicitor when you call them, and get permission to use their name when you contact the other people.]

[If your company offers an incentive for referrals, discuss this inducement for providing names. If they don't have any names now but agree to help you, set up a time to call them to get their referrals.]

"By the way, let me give you some of my business cards so you'll have them available if you're talking to anyone that you think I should meet. And if you can, let me who you gave one to."

"Also, I'd like to send you our newsletter (specials, updates) on a periodic basis just so you will be aware of what we're offering. Is email OK?" [Wait for the response.]

[Confirm their email address or determine which one to use. You can also email them your contact information or vCard and send them a link to your website and blog, if you have one.]

[Discuss your next contact and agree on when and where that is to be and if it's going to be by email, phone, or in-person. You might set a time to get together for breakfast or coffee depending on how close your offices are to each other and how appropriate your product or service is for them or their circle of contacts.]

"I'll talk to (see) you again then. Really great talking to you. Thanks for your help. Good-bye."

An Unexpected Meeting With A Friend

Use this scenario to talk with a friend or acquaintance that you happen to see unexpectedly someplace in public — regardless of how well you know them or how long it's been since you've seen or talked with them. Use this unplanned and impromptu meeting to reestablish and renew your relationship. You want to make sure they know what you're doing now and mention to them that you can use their help in finding people interested in what you offer. You may not be able to accomplish all of this in a brief, chance encounter. A subsequent phone call, email, or another meeting might be required.

———

"Hi, <first name of friend that you meet in public>."

[After you exchange greetings and catch up on what each other has been doing, trade business cards if the contact information has changed. Hand out yours anyway. This may be the extent of what you can accomplish during this brief meeting.]

[If your friend that you are meeting does not have a card, be prepared to write down his or her contact information or have them write it for you on the back of one of your business cards. If you have them write down the information for you, be sure to inspect what they have provided, make sure you can read all of it, and confirm it with them. You know their name, but their preferred phone number and email is what you really need to get.]

JUST A BRIEF CONVERSATION — *"I'd really like to learn more about what you are doing these days and have a chance to tell you about what we're doing. I possibly could use your help."*

"When would it be convenient for me to call you so we could talk some more or schedule a time to grab a cup of coffee?" [Wait for response and agree on a day and time for the call or meeting.]

"Great, I'll call you <day and time agreed on>."

"Nice seeing you again. Good-bye."

A LONGER CONVERSATION — *"I'd really like to learn more about what you are doing these days."* [Let him or her talk, listen to what they say, and ask questions — pay particular attention to the types of people he or she might know or the clientele served to frame your question for referrals.]

"I represent <name of your company> (I have my own business) at <provide the actual location, address, or general description of the area — whatever would make the most sense to your friend>?"

"We offer (provide) <brief description of products, services, solutions, or opportunities you have — especially ones that might interest or connect with your friend or his or her business>."

[Be careful not to share too much information about your opportunity. You are not trying to deliver a "mini-presentation" even though it might be tempting to do so. You just want to provide a basic description of what you offer so that you establish a frame of reference.]

"I thought that maybe you personally or possibly you might know or have heard of someone (two or three people) that might be in the market for what we (I) provide and that you or they should take a look at (hear about, consider) what we have to offer." [Wait for response.]

[If he or she indicates any kind of interest — for them individually or for their business, depending on what you offer — arrange another time to meet and discuss it in more detail.]

"Who comes to mind (Can you think of one or two people) that falls into this category? (Who is the first

person who comes to mind when I ask this question?)"
[Wait for a response.]

[If he or she readily volunteers a name or two, write it down and ask for a way to contact that person or persons. Be sure to note the correct spelling and pronunciation. Get first names so you don't sound like a telemarketer or solicitor, and get permission to use your friend's name when you contact the other people they are furnishing. If your company offers an incentive for referrals, discuss this inducement for providing names.]

They Have Names to Give You — *"That's great. I will call them and discuss what we offer and see where it goes from there. Then, I will call you after I have spoken with them to let you know what happened."*

"Can you think of anyone else?" [Wait for response.] *"Thanks for your help. Great seeing you again."*

"By the way, if you don't mind, let me give you some of my business cards so you'll have them available if you're talking to anyone that you think I should meet. And if you can, let me who was interested enough to take my card or who you gave one to."

"Good-bye."

No Names to Give You at This Time — *"That's quite all right."*

"I'd like to keep in touch with you and send you our newsletter (updates, specials) on a periodic basis just so you will be aware of what we're offering. Is email OK to use?" [Wait for the response. Confirm their email address or determine which one to use. You can also send them your contact information or vCard and send them a link to your website and blog, if you have one.]

"Fine. If anyone does come to mind that you think should know about what we offer, let me know and we'll take it from there."

"In fact, let me give you some of my business cards so you'll have them available if you're talking to anyone that you think I should meet."

"If you can, let me know who was interested enough to take my card or who you gave one to."

"Would you have a place where I could leave some of my business cards or put out a small display?" [Wait for response, and accept the answer either way.]

"Thanks for your help. See you again next time. Good-bye."

Planned Visit With A Friend

Use this scenario to talk with a friend of yours when you drop into their office to meet with them or visit them at a location where you know they'll be such as their kid's ballgame, a tent sale, a trade show booth, a charity car wash, or similar event or location. Use this to renew your relationship — especially if it's been a while since you've seen or talked with them. You want to make sure they know what you're doing now and you want to determine an initial interest in possible hearing about what you offer. You'd also like their help in identifying other people that might be interested in what you offer. You may not be able to accomplish all of this during an unscheduled visit, so a subsequent phone call, email, or meeting might be required.

———

"Hi, <first name of your friend>."

[Exchange greetings, learn what each other has been doing since you last talked, and trade business cards.]

[Your friend should have a business card, but if they don't, be prepared to write down their contact information on the back of one of your cards. If you have them write the information, be sure to check it, make sure you can read all of it, and confirm it with them.]

JUST A BRIEF CONVERSATION — *"I'd really like to hear more about how you're doing these days and have a chance to tell you about what we're doing. And I sure could use your help."*

"When would be a convenient (good) time for us to have coffee (talk again)?" [Wait for response, determine which they prefer, and agree on the day, time, and location for the call or visit.] *"Great. I'll call (see) you <day and time agreed on>. Nice seeing you again. Good-bye."*

A LONGER CONVERSATION — *"I'd really like to hear more about your business and how you're doing these days. I'd also like to tell you a little bit about what we're doing."*

[Let him or her talk, listen to what they say, and ask questions about their business and their market experiences — pay particular attention to the types of people he or she might know or the clientele served to frame your question for referrals.]

"I'm with <name of your company> (I have my own business) and we offer (provide) <brief description of what you have — especially ones that might interest or connect with your friend or his or her business>."

[Be careful not to share too much information about your opportunity. You are not trying to deliver a "mini-presentation" even though it might be tempting to do so. You just want to provide a basic description of what you offer so that you establish a frame of reference.]

"I thought that maybe you personally or possibly you might know or have heard of someone (two or three

people) that might be in the market for what we (I) provide and that you or they should take a look at (hear about, consider) what we have to offer." [Wait for response.]

[If he or she indicates any kind of interest — for them individually or for their business, depending on what you offer — arrange another time to meet and discuss it in more detail.]

"Who comes to mind (Can you think of one or two people) that falls into this category? (Who is the first person who comes to mind when I ask this question?)" [Wait for a response.]

[If he or she readily volunteers a name or two, write it down and ask for a way to contact that person or persons. Be sure to note the correct spelling and pronunciation. Get first names so you don't sound like a telemarketer or solicitor, and get permission to use your friend's name when you contact the other people they are furnishing. If your company offers an incentive for referrals, discuss this inducement for providing names.]

They Have Names to Give You — *"That's great. I will call them and discuss what we offer and see where it goes from there. Then, I will call you after I have spoken with them to let you know what happened."*

"Can you think of anyone else?" [Wait for response.]

"Thanks for your help. Great seeing you again."

"By the way, if you don't mind, let me give you some of my business cards so you'll have them available if you're talking to anyone that you think I should meet. And if you can, let me who was interested enough to take my card or who you gave one to."

"Good-bye."

No Names to Give You at This Time — *"That's quite all right."*

"I'd like to keep in touch with you and send you our newsletter (updates, specials) on a periodic basis just so you will be aware of what we're offering. Is email OK to use?" [Wait for the response. Confirm their email address or determine which one to use. You can also send them your contact information or vCard and send them a link to your website and blog, if you have one.]

"Fine. If anyone does come to mind that you think should know about what we offer, let me know and we'll take it from there."

"In fact, let me give you some of my business cards so you'll have them available if you're talking to anyone that you think I should meet. If you can, let me know who was interested enough to take my card or who you gave one to."

"Thanks for your help. See you again next time. Good-bye."

Visit With Your Regular Delivery People

Use this scenario to talk with delivery people that you know because you are their customer or on their route —UPS, FedEx, USPS, office supply, bottled water, coffee service, or other messenger, freight, or parcel delivery service that visit your office, home office, or home on a regular basis — to ask for their help. You may not be able to accomplish that much due to their delivery schedules that they have to keep, so an ensuing phone call or email — or waiting until the next visit — might be required.

———

"Hi, <first name of delivery person that you see on a regular basis>."

[You may not have much time for small talk due to their schedules. If you do fine, but be prepared to get right to your message.]

"I'd like your help on (with) something."

"As you may know (probably know), we offer <a basic description of what type of product, service, or opportunity you provide>, but I don't know (think) that we've ever talked that much about it."

"Would you like (Do you have time) to hear a little bit more about what we do so that you can help me identify some people that you know that might be able to take advantage of (be in the market for) what we provide?"

Yes — *"Great."* [Determine how much time they have and stick to it. Give them the basic details of what you do and how you need their help.]

No — *"That's quite all right."*

"I wondered who you might know or might have heard of in your travels who is in the market for what we provide and should take a look at (hear about, consider) what we have to offer." [Wait for response.]

[If you provide consumer products or in-home or at-home services, they may indicate that they would be interested in learning more for their personal use.]

[They may need to let you know later or require some time to think about it, but if he or she readily volunteers a name or two now, write it down and ask for a way to contact them.]

[Be sure to note the correct spelling and pronunciation. Get first names so you don't sound like a telemarketer or solicitor, and get permission to use the person's name that is giving you the referrals when you contact the other people.]

They Have Names to Give You — *"That's great. I will call them and talk with them briefly about what we offer and take it from there (see if there is any interest)."*

"The next time you drop by I'll tell you what happened."

"Can you think of anyone else?" [Wait for response.]

"Thanks. I appreciate your help. See you next time. Have a great day."

"By the way, if you don't mind, let me give you some of my business cards so you'll have them available if you're talking to anyone that you think should learn about what we do (offer, provide). If you can, let me who you give them to."

"Thanks again. Good-bye."

No Names to Give You at This Time — *"That's quite all right. Thanks for trying. Maybe next time."*

"If anyone comes to mind that you think should know about what we provide (offer), you can tell them about what we're doing, or you can let me know who they are whenever you come in and I'll take it from there (give them a call)."

"In fact, if you don't mind, let me give you some of my business cards so you'll have them available if you're

talking to anyone that you think I should meet (see what we're doing). If you can, let me who you give them to."

"I really appreciate your help. See you again next time. Have a good one. Good-bye."

Visit With Your Regular
Service & Repair People

Use this scenario to talk with people you know who visit you at your office, home, or home office on a regular basis to ask for their help during one of their scheduled visits. This would include your computer technician, copier repair technician, regular phone technician or electrician, the people who take care of your indoor plants, the outside landscapers and yard service, the cleaning crew, and other service or technical people that work with you and your company on a regular basis. You may not be able to accomplish much during a single conversation due to their schedules, so a subsequent phone call or email — or waiting until their next visit — might be required.

———

"Hi, <first name of service or repair person that you see on a regular basis>. I'd like your help on (with) something."

[You may have time for a little small talk, but be prepared to get right to your message.]

"As you may know (probably know), we offer <a basic description of what type of product, service, or opportunity you provide>, but I don't know (think) that we've ever talked that much about it."

"Would you like (Do you have time) to hear a little bit more about what we do so that you can help me identify some people that you know that might be able to take advantage of (be in the market for) what we provide?"

Yes — *"Great."* [Determine how much time they have and stick to it. Give them the basic details of what you do and how you need their help. Be careful not to interfere with their work or to complicate what they are doing by distracting them.]

No — *"That's quite all right."*

"I wondered who you might know or might have heard of in your travels who is in the market for what we provide and should take a look at (hear about, consider) what we have to offer." [Wait for response.]

[If you provide consumer products or in-home or at-home services, they may indicate that they would be interested in learning more for their personal use.]

[They may need to let you know later or require some time to think about it, but if he or she readily volunteers a name or two now, write it down and ask for a way to contact them. Be sure to note the correct spelling and pronunciation. Get first names so you don't sound like a telemarketer or solicitor, and get permission to use the person's name that is giving you the referrals when you contact the other people.]

They Have Names to Give You — *"That's great. I will call them and talk with them briefly about what we offer and take it from there (see if there is any interest)."*

"On your next scheduled visit I'll tell you what happened. Can you think of anyone else?" [Wait for response.]

"Thanks. I appreciate your help. See you next time. Have a great day."

"By the way, if you don't mind, let me give you some of my business cards so you'll have them available if you're talking to anyone that you think should learn about what we do (offer, provide). If you can, let me who you give them to."

"Thanks again. Good-bye."

No Names to Give You at This Time — *"That's quite all right. Thanks for trying. Maybe next time."*

"If anyone comes to mind that you think should know about what we provide (offer), you can tell them

about what we're doing, or you can let me know who they are whenever you come in and I'll take it from there (give them a call)."

"In fact, if you don't mind, let me give you some of my business cards so you'll have them available if you're talking to anyone that you think should see what we're doing. If you can, let me who you give them to."

"I really appreciate your help. See you again next time. Have a good one. Good-bye."

Conversation With People At A Special Event Or Trade Show

Use this scenario to talk with someone you have talked with and already gotten to know briefly who has just finished looking at your products or display during a special event like an open house, an off-site display like a kiosk, or a trade show or home expo. Whether they seem to have a specific interest in what you are offering or not, ask for their help to determine if there are others that they can lead you to who should look at or know about what you provide.

———

[After discussing your products, services, solutions, or opportunities, answering their questions, conducting your discovery, and engaging in small talk, turn the conversation to this.]

"Many people, after they see (hear about, learn about) what we have to offer, say, 'Gee, I wish so-and-so could have seen this (heard about this, was here to see this). This would be perfect for them (for what they are looking for),' or 'I wish Fred and Linda had been here to see this. This is exactly what they're looking for (interested in, been talking about)."

[Look to see if they nod agreement or listen for verbal confirmation or an indication that they have been feeling this sentiment.]

"Who comes to mind that you've been thinking this about as I have been talking with you about what we offer?" [Wait for a response.]

[If they volunteer a name or two, write it down and ask for a way to contact that person or persons. Be sure to note the correct spelling and pronunciation. Get first names so you don't sound like a telemarketer or solicitor, and get permission to use the person's name that is giving you the referrals when you contact the other people. If your company offers an incentive for referrals, discuss this inducement for providing names.]

They Have Names to Give You — *"That's great. I will call them and invite them to take a look at what we offer (provide)."*

"Can you think of anyone else?" [Wait for response.]

"Thanks for your help. I really appreciate it."

"In fact, if you don't mind, let me give you some of my business cards so you'll have them available if you're talking to anyone that you think should see what we offer."

"Just have them mention your name when they contact me or let me know who they are. If you like, you can call (email) me to tell me who to watch for."

[Continue with your presentation, including setting and agreeing on the next contact.]

No Names to Give You at This Time — *"That's quite all right. Thanks for trying."*

"By the way, if anyone comes to mind that you think should know about what we do, you can tell me the next time we talk and I'll take it from there."

"In fact, if you don't mind, let me give you some of my business cards so you'll have them available if you're talking to anyone that you think should see what we offer. Just have them mention your name when they contact me or let me know who they are. If you like, you can call (email) me to tell me who to watch for."

[Continue with your presentation, including setting and agreeing on the next contact.]

Conversation With Interested People
After A Presentation

Use this scenario to continue your conversation with someone who seems to like what they have seen and heard when you finish your presentation to them — in their office, your office or showroom, their home, or elsewhere — to ask for their help while you're still together and they are excited about what you have described. Besides trying to make a sale with them, you want to learn if there are other people that they can lead you to who should look at what you are offering.

———

[After discussing what you offer, and getting a favorable response — either before or after your final closing question — turn your conversation toward referrals.]

"Many people, after they see what we have to offer, say, 'Gee, I wish so-and-so could see this. This would be perfect for them (for what they are looking for)' or 'I wish Fred and Linda had been here with us to see this. This is exactly what they're looking for (interested in, what they've been talking about)' or 'I wish my cousin could have been here to see this because this is exactly what he needs for his business."

[Look to see if they nod agreement or listen for verbal confirmation or an indication that they have been feeling this sentiment.]

"Who have you been saying this about as I have been talking the past few minutes?" [Wait for a response.]

[If they volunteer a name or two, write it down and ask for a way to contact that person or persons. Be sure to note the correct spelling and pronunciation. Get first names so you don't sound like a telemarketer or solicitor, and get permission to use the person's name that is giving you the referrals when you contact the other people. If your company offers an incentive for referrals, discuss this inducement for providing names.]

They Have Names to Give You — *"That's great. I will call them and talk with them briefly to see if there is any interest. Then I'll take it from there."*

"The next time we talk, I'll let you know what they had to say and if they seemed to like what we are offering as much as you think they will."

"Can you think of anyone else?" [Wait for response.]

"Thanks for your help. I really appreciate it."

"In fact, if you don't mind, let me give you some of my business cards so you'll have them available if you're talking to anyone that you think should see what we're doing. Just have them mention your name when they contact me or let me know who they are. If you like, you can call (email) me to tell me who to watch for."

[Continue with your presentation, including setting and agreeing on the next contact or asking for the sale again.] *"Good-bye."* [Remind them of your next contact.]

No Names to Give You at This Time — *"That's quite all right. Thanks for trying. Maybe the next time we talk."*

"By the way, if anyone comes to mind that you think should know about what we're offering (providing, doing), you can tell me the next time we talk and I'll invite them to take a look."

"In fact, if you don't mind, let me give you some of my business cards so you'll have them if you're talking to anyone that you think should see what we offer. Just have them mention your name when they contact me or let me know who they are. If you like, you can call (email) me to tell me who to watch for."

[Continue with your presentation, including setting and agreeing on the next contact or closing again.]

"Good-bye." [Remind them of your next contact.]

Conversation With Uninterested People After A Presentation

Use this scenario to continue your conversation with someone who does not seem to like (for whatever reason) what they have seen and heard after you finish making your presentation to them — in their office, your office or showroom, their home, or elsewhere — to ask for their help while they're still in your presence and what you described is still fresh. You want to determine if there are other people that they can lead you to who should look at what you are offering.

———

[After conducting your sales presentation and determining that they are not going to be agreeing to your proposal — but prior to saying good-bye to them — turn your conversation toward asking for referrals.]

"I really have enjoyed our time together today (this morning, tonight), and I'm sorry that you don't think we can meet your needs (you don't think this will work for you), but let me ask you this."

"Obviously, different people and companies [depending on what you're offering and who your audience is] *have different needs, so there's probably at least one person or couple (company, business, business friend) that you can think of right now — or that came to mind as we were discussing what we can do — who might like to hear about what we have to offer or really should take a look at what you just saw?"* [Wait for response.]

"Who have you thought of that you think would enjoy learning about (should hear about) what we offer?" [Wait for a response.]

[If no response or a negative one, try this.] *"Even though you don't think this is a good solution for you, perhaps as I was talking about what we offer you were thinking (saying to yourself) 'Gee, I wish so-and-so could see this. This would be perfect for them (for what they are looking for)' or 'I wish Fred and Linda had been here with us to see this. This is exactly what they're looking for (interested in, what they've been talking about)' or 'I wish my cousin could have been here to see this because this is exactly what he needs for his business. "* [Look to see if they nod agreement or listen for verbal confirmation or an indication that they have been feeling this sentiment.]

"Who have you been saying (thinking) this about as I have been talking the past few minutes?" [Wait for a response.]

[If they volunteer a name or two, write it down and then ask for a way to contact that person or persons. Be sure to note the correct spelling and pronunciation of each name, and get their first names so you don't sound like a telemarketer or solicitor, and get permission to use the person's name that is giving you the referrals when you contact the other people. If your company offers an incentive for referrals, discuss this inducement for providing names.]

They Have Names to Give You — *"That's great. I will call them and talk with them briefly to see if there is any interest in going further."*

"*Can you think of anyone else?*" [Wait for response.] "*Thanks for your help. I really appreciate it.*"

"*In fact, if you don't mind, let me give you some of my business cards if you're talking to anyone that you think should see what we offer.*"

"*Just have them mention your name when they contact me or let me know who they are. If you like, you can call (email) me to tell me who to watch for. Good-bye, and thanks for meeting with me.*"

No Names to Give You at This Time — "*That's quite all right. Thanks for trying. By the way, if anyone comes to mind that you think should know about what we offer, please let me know.*"

"*In fact, if you don't mind, let me give you some of my business cards so you'll have them available if you're talking to anyone that you think should see what we're doing. Just have them mention your name when they contact me or let me know who they are.*"

"*Good-bye, and thanks for talking with me.*"

Conversation With A New Purchaser

Use this scenario to talk with someone who has purchased a product or service from you or agreed to join your organization. This can be used at the time of the purchase agreement, at delivery, at installation, or any other time immediately following the buying decision. You are looking for people that they know that they haven't already told you about that you can talk to about what you offer.

———

[After discussing the other issues that you needed to address — and making sure that everything is correct with the order — turn your conversation toward asking for referrals.]

"*Now that you have decided that <name or description of your product or service or the name of your organization in the case of a membership opportunity> is what you want, I am sure that you can think of several of your friends or associates that could benefit from what we offer as well.*" [Watch for a nod or listen for verbal confirmation or agreement.]

"*Who are the first two or three people who come to mind that you think really ought to look at what we have to offer?*" [Wait for a response.]

[Be prepared to write down any names they give you (or give them a card that they can use for this purpose) and ask for a way to contact those people they tell you about that they think might interested in looking at your homes. Be sure to note the correct spelling and pronunciation. Get first names so you don't sound like a telemarketer or solicitor. Get permission to use your purchaser's name(s) when you contact the other people.]

[If your company offers an incentive for referrals — especially from new purchasers, discuss this inducement for providing names.]

They Have Names to Give You — *"That's great."*

"I'll invite them to look at what we have to offer, and I'll let you know what happened."

"Can you think of anyone else?" [Wait for response.]

"Thanks for your help. I really appreciate it." [Continue with your conversation.]

"By the way, let me give you some of my business cards so you'll have them available if you're talking to anyone that you think should see what we're doing. Just have them mention your name when they contact me or let me know who they are so I can look out for them. If you like, you can call (email) me to tell me who to watch for, or you can even bring them by. Good-bye."

No Names to Give You at This Time — *"That's quite all right."*

"You'll probably think of some later on, and you can tell me about them the next time we talk or even email

them to me. Then I'll call them and discuss what we offer to see if there is any interest in going further."

"By the way, let me give you some of my business cards so you'll have them available if you're talking to anyone that you think should see what we offer (provide, do). Just have them mention your name when they contact me or let me know who they are so I can look out for them. If you like, you can call (email) me to tell me who to watch for, or you can even bring them by."

[Continue with your conversation.] *"Good-bye."*

Conversation With An Established Customer

Use this scenario to talk with someone that you know that has been using your product or service or belonged to your organization for several months. You might see them in public, they might return to your showroom or sales center, or you might call upon them at their business or home (depending on the type of product or service that you offer) to talk about how you can use their help.

———

[Greet them and exchange small talk. Pick out something specific to highlight or compliment them on.]

"I really appreciate the confidence you have shown in

us by *(deciding upon, using, purchasing) one of our <name of product>/allowing us to provide <name or description of service> for you. It means a lot to me, and I really could use your help."*

"You know what our product (services) have done for you (what a difference our <name or description of product or service> has made for you), so who are the first two or three names that come to mind that you think would like to know about what we offer and how it can help them?" [Wait for a response.]

[Be prepared to write down any names they give you and ask for a way to contact those people. Be sure to note the correct spelling and pronunciation. Get first names so you don't sound like a telemarketer or solicitor. Get permission to use your resident's name(s) when you contact the other people. If your company offers an incentive to residents for referrals, discuss this inducement for providing names.]

They Have Names to Give You — *"That's great. I'll call and discuss what we have to offer, and the next time we talk I'll let you know what happened. Can you think of anyone else?"* [Wait for response.]

"Thanks for your help. I really appreciate it."

"By the way, let me give you some of my business cards so you'll have them available if you're talking to

anyone that you think should see what we offer. Just have them mention your name when they contact me or let me know who they are so I'll be sure to look out for them. If you like, you can call (email, stop by) to tell me who to watch for, or you can even bring them by."

[Continue with your conversation.] "Good-bye. Have a great day."

No Names to Give You at This Time — "That's quite all right. Thanks for trying. Maybe another time."

"I'm sure you'll think of some people later on, and you can tell me who they are the next time we talk or you can drop by the office or email me. Then I'll contact them and invite them to consider what we offer so they can experience what you already know."

"By the way, let me give you some of my business cards so you'll have them available if you're talking to anyone that you think should see what we offer. Just have them mention your name when they contact me or let me know who they are so I'll be sure to look out for them. If you like, you can call (email, stop by) to tell me who to watch for, or you can even bring them by."

[Continue with your conversation.] "Good-bye and have a great day."

Conversation With A Referring
Client Or Customer

Use this scenario to talk with a client or customer of yours who already has furnished you with referrals — to thank them for furnishing you with leads in the past and to request their help again.

———

[Greet them and exchange small talk. Pick out something specific to compliment them on or highlight.]

"*I really value your trust and confidence that you have shown in us by owning (using) one of our <name of product>/allowing us to provide <name or description of service> for you. It means a lot to me.*"

"*You've already given me the names of several (many, one, two, a couple) of your friends (former neighbors, relatives, colleagues, co-workers, associates) and have allowed me to contact them to let them know about what we offer and how we might be able to help them.*"

"*I really appreciate your help, but I still can use your assistance.*"

"*We all meet new people all the time — or think of ones that we hadn't thought of before — so in addition to people that you've already told me about, I thought*"

I'd check with you to see which two or three people you might have met recently or that you hadn't thought about before that you think should know about what we offer." [Wait for response.]

[Be prepared to write down any names they give you and ask for a way to contact those people. Be sure to note the correct spelling and pronunciation. Get first names so you don't sound like a telemarketer or solicitor. Get permission to use your resident's name(s) when you contact the other people. If your company offers an incentive for referrals, discuss this — especially if it's a new policy.]

They Have Names to Give You — "That's great. I'll contact them like I did the others you told me about and see what type of interest they might have. The next time we talk I'll let you know what happened."

"Can you think of anyone else?" [Wait for response.] "Thanks for your help. I really appreciate it."

"By the way, let me give you some more of my business cards so you'll have them available for anyone that you think should know about what we offer. Just let me know who they are so I'll be sure to look out for them."

[Continue with your conversation.] "Good-bye and have a great day."

No Names to Give You at This Time — *"That's quite all right. Thanks for trying. Maybe the next time."*

"I'm sure you'll probably think of some more people later on, and you can tell me who they are the next time we talk or you can drop by the office or email me (give me a call). Then I'll contact them like I did before and discuss what we offer with them."

"By the way, let me give you some more of my business cards so you'll have them available for anyone that you think should know about what we offer. Just let me know who they are so I'll be sure to look out for them."

[Continue with your conversation.] *"Good-bye and have a great day."*

5

Connecting By Telephone

The Value Of Telephone Contact

Planned, or even impromptu, in-person meetings and conversations are great for interacting and connecting with friends and acquaintances.

Smiles, shrugs, hand gestures, grins, chuckles, laughs, raised eyebrows, a touch, rolling of the eyes, surprised or shocked looks, anger, disgust, frustration, elation, frowns, confusion, empathy, and other expressions of emotion are immediately conveyed during a face-to-face meeting or conversation.

However, that type of contact — as ideal as it is — isn't always necessary, available, or convenient. The person you want to talk with could be hundreds or even thousands of miles away.

Therefore, the next best thing to talking to someone in-person is speaking to them by phone.

The telephone is a powerful way of reaching out and staying connected with your circle of contacts.

While you can't see what each other is saying and how you are communicating your message (unless you're using something like Skype, webcams, or FaceTime), you still get to hear each other and often can sense how the other is speaking — particularly if you know them fairly well.

Your "Circle Of Contacts"

All of us know people from a variety of sources — family, school, former employers and employees, colleagues, customers, current and former neighborhoods, church, clubs, organizations, community and civic groups, recreational activities, charities, local businesses and professionals, and friends of our kids and spouse.

Many people refer to this network of friends, family, and associates that we have as our "sphere of influence," "circle of friends," or "circle of influence," but I don't think these are great terms to use.

Rather, I use a more inclusive term that applies to all the people we know — regardless of how we met them, how well we might know them, how long we have known them, and when we last spoke to them.

Therefore, I simply call it our "circle of contacts."

Undoubtedly, you have a database of your contacts stored as a stack of business cards in your rolodex or in a drawer, a more formal arrangement of them in your computer in a CRM (contact relational manager) such as ACT! or Outlook, in your PDA, on your smartphone, or on more than one of these.

Anytime you want, you can pick up the telephone and reach out to any of your contacts. You probably even have the numbers of the people you call the most memorized, on speed dial, or in your favorites.

The nice thing about using the phone to contact people is that you don't have to get in your car or leave your home or office. No special preparation is required other than what you want to say and who you want to call.

You Know Many People

In addition to your family, neighbors, close friends, colleagues, associates, and others you see or socialize with on a regular basis, there are many other business contacts that you can rely upon to help you generate leads and build your business.

These include other salespeople in your market that you have a good relationship with and that you're not in direct competition with, residential and commercial Realtors® that you know, professionals such as attorneys and physicians you use in your market area, and lenders and mortgage brokers that you have worked with.

You also have names and phone numbers for appraisers, home inspectors, interior decorators, home stagers, suppliers, tradespeople, businesses that you patronize, entertainment and recreational facilities you use, governmental offices where you know people, and restaurants in your area that you patronize.

Add to that the customers you've sold your products and services to and the ones you're still working with to help them make a decision.

Your data bank is full of names and phone numbers.

Getting Started

All you need to do is begin tapping into this major resource as you reach out and connect with people you already know and ask for their help.

You need sales and referrals, and they can help you. They want to help you. You just need to ask and make them aware of what you need.

We already addressed calling on people in-person or seeing them in public. This chapter focuses specifically on using the telephone to connect with people that you already know in some way.

I'm talking specifically about connecting by phone with people that you already know and that you know well enough — even if you haven't seen or spoken with them in a while — to be able to pick up the phone, call them, and have them take your call and speak with you.

There's no reason for concern.

You're calling your friends — or at least people that you have met along the way — who know who you are and will recognize your name when you call them.

Not everyone may agree to help or feel that they are capable of helping you, but your request is legitimate and is not based on testing or taking advantage of your friendship.

Tapping Into A Willingness

In this chapter, I give you some suggested language to use for your telephone conversations as you reach out to people that can help you. Use it as-is or as a guide.

Just remember that the people you are calling are not strangers. Some you will know better than others, and some longer than others. However, there is no reason not to call them and ask for their help.

People like to help you if they know what you need and feel that it's something they can do.

It's human nature to want to help someone if we feel that we can and that we won't be too inconvenienced by doing so.

You just need to ask the people you're calling for their help and make them aware of what you need. Then reassure them that they have the ability to help you.

Call After A Brief Introduction

Use this scenario for your telephone call the day after or soon after meeting someone initially and talking briefly with them at a business or social function or in public. Primarily you want to talk with them some more or set up a meeting with them to determine if they have an interest in what you offer and who they might know that has an interest in what you provide.

"Hello <use their first name>? This is <your name> from <name of your company>."

"I met you <last night, Tuesday, yesterday, the other day, last week, or recently> at the <mention the

specific event or place where you met, such as chamber of commerce breakfast, church, Little League game, the mall, a specific store or restaurant, the Rotary Club, etc.> and we met just long enough to exchange business cards and that was about it."

"Do you have a quick minute?" [Wait for response.]

NOW IS NOT A GOOD TIME — [You actually speak to your new friend or acquaintance, but they are unable to devote any additional time to you now.] "No problem. Let me call back when you have a minute."

"Then we can schedule a convenient (good) time for me to could stop by to meet with you for a few minutes." [Set up a convenient time to talk again, but do not set up the appointment to meet unless they insist and will talk long enough to set that future appointment but no more.] "Good-bye."

HAS JUST A QUICK MINUTE NOW — [You actually get to speak to the person you are calling, but they don't have much time to talk — just set an appointment for the next contact.]

"Great. I'll make this quick. I just wanted to call to say hello again and to set a convenient (good) time when I could stop by for a couple of minutes to learn a little bit more about your business (what you do) and let you know who we are."

[If you told them when you met that you would call to set up a time to meet, mention this.] *"Maybe you'd let me buy you a cup of coffee. Which one is better for you <meeting at their office or a coffee shop>?"* [Wait for response.]

"Fine." [Agree on the place, date, and time].

"Thanks. I look forward to seeing you again on <date of the appointment> at <agreed time> at <agreed location>."

"Would you like for me to email you a reminder?" [Wait for response.]

Yes — *"Fine. I'll send you a note on <specific day> to remind you of our appointment on <day, time, and location>. Which email address should I use?"* [Confirm the address or write it down as you obtain it.]

"I look forward to seeing (meeting) you then (again). Good-bye."

No — *"Fine. I'll plan on seeing you then on <mention the day and time> at <place>. Good-bye."*

Call To A Social Networking Contact

Use this scenario to call any person that you know through social networking sites because you have commented on their site or connected with them online sufficiently that they know who you are. You mainly want to talk with them — rather than set a meeting — to determine who they know who has an interest in buying something you offer that they can refer to you. Call them on their cell phone to avoid office voice mail and "screeners." They may be miles away from your area. Depending on what you offer and how easily your product, service, or solution is shipped, transported, delivered, or installed, they might be a candidate for what you offer also.

———

"Hello <use their first name>? This is <your name>."

"I know you from <name of networking site where you both are a member>." [The person you are calling should immediately recognize your name.]

NOW IS NOT A GOOD TIME — *"No problem. I know you weren't expecting my call right now. Let me call back when you have a minute."* [Set up a convenient time to talk again.]

"I'll give you a call again on <date agreed, and possibly set a specific time as well>. Good-bye."

IS AVAILABLE NOW — *"Great. I'll make this fairly quick."*

"As you may (probably) know, I sell <name of general

product or service and if it is confined to a particular market area or not>. I thought maybe you could help me identify people who might be interested in looking for <what you offer> in my area (their area if you service it) — now or in the near future."

[Listen for their general willingness to help you. If he or she mentions that they might have an interest or that they would like to help you, set up another call at a mutually convenient time. If they volunteer a name or two, write it down and ask for a way to contact that person or persons. Be sure to note the correct spelling and pronunciation. Get first names so you don't sound like a telemarketer or solicitor when you call them, and get permission to use their name when you contact the other people. If there seems to be no interest in helping you or in establishing a professional relationship, conclude the call.]

"Thanks for taking my call. Good-bye. See you online."

Call To A Friend Or Acquaintance

Use this scenario to call and talk with someone you know very well or well enough to speak to each other and have a conversation when you meet. You want to make sure they know what your current role is and that you want to enlist their help in identifying people that they know (even if it's them) that might be interested in looking at or purchasing what you offer.

"Hi, <first name or nickname of your friend>. This is <your name — possibly just your first name>. I wasn't sure if you were aware that I am (began) working with <name of your company or brand group> (started my own company> and we're located at <a general description is probably enough>."

"I'd really like to catch up with you and learn more about your business and what you do and get a chance to tell you about what we are (I am) doing. Also, I possibly could use your help."

"Do you have some now or would it be better for me to call back at a better time?" [Wait for response.]

Now Is OK — *"Fine."* [Discuss what your friend is doing. You also can set a time to get together for breakfast or coffee depending on how close your offices are to each other. Then talk about what you are doing. Listen for an indication of interest.]

"I mentioned that I can use your help. I thought maybe you might have an interest in what we offer, but if not, I could use your help identifying people who might be interested in looking at (for) <name or description of product or service you provide> in my area (your area) — now or in the near future. Possibly some people that you know that I don't."

[If there seems to be reluctance or no interest in helping

you or in developing a professional relationship, conclude the call and do not call them again for referrals.]

"Who are the first couple of names that come to mind right now that you think would take my call to let them know about what we (I) offer?" [Wait for response.]

[If they volunteer a name or two, write it down and ask for a way to contact that person or persons. Be sure to note the correct spelling and pronunciation. Get first names so you don't sound like a telemarketer or solicitor when you call them, and get permission to use their name when you contact the other people. If you or your company offers an incentive for referrals, discuss this inducement for providing names.]

"I'd like to send you our newsletter (updates, specials) on a periodic basis just so you will be aware of what we're offering. Is email OK?" [Wait for the response. Confirm their email address or determine which one to use. You can also send them your contact information or vCard and send them a link to your website and blog, if you have one. Then, discuss your next contact and agree on when and where that is to be and if it's by email, phone, or in-person.]

"I'll talk to (see) you again then. Really great talking to you. Thanks for your time. Good-bye."

NOW IS NOT A GOOD TIME — *"I knew that you might be*

busy and that you weren't expecting my call right now (that you might not have time to talk right now), but I thought I'd take a chance."

"Let me call back when you have a minute (a few minutes) for us to talk." [Set up a convenient time to talk again.]

"Talk to you then. Good-bye."

Call From A Friend Or Acquaintance

Use this scenario to talk with a friend or acquaintance when they call you for whatever reason — someone you know very well or well enough to speak to each other and have a conversation when you meet or call each other. They will be calling you on your cell phone since the presumption is that they don't know where you are working. You might recognize their phone number or their voice. You want to make sure they know what your current role is — should they have a need for what you offer or provide — and you want to enlist their help in identifying people that they know that might be interested in looking at what you offer.

[Answer the phone. Hear the other person identify themselves — unless you recognize their voice or your phone displays their name.] "Hi, <first name or nickname of your friend>."

[Listen to them and discuss what they want to talk about with you — after all, they are initiating the call. Then at an appropriate moment, if there is one, change gears and use the conversation to talk about what you want. If they can't stay on the call, or the reason for the call or the tone of the conversation doesn't seem appropriate for you to get into a business discussion, tell them you will call them back later to talk some more.]

"*I recently began working with <name of your company> (just/recently started my own business) and we're located at <a general description is probably enough>.*" [Talk briefly about what you offer.]

[Listen for their general willingness to help you. If he or she mentions that they might have an interest or that they would like to help you, set up another call at a mutually convenient time.]

[If there seems to be no interest in what you offer or in helping you locate people who might have an interest in what you offer — or in establishing a strategic relationship — change the subject or conclude the call.]

Now Is OK — "*Fine. I thought maybe you might have an interest in what we offer, but if not, I could use your help identifying people who might be interested in looking at (for) <name or description of product or service you provide> in my area (your area) — now or in the near future. Possibly some people that you know* *that I don't."*

"Who are the first couple of names — even you —that come to mind right now that you think would be interested in hearing more about what we offer?"

[Wait for response. If they volunteer a name or two, write it down and ask for a way to contact that person or persons. Be sure to note the correct spelling and pronunciation. Get first names so you don't sound like a telemarketer or solicitor when you call them, and get permission to use their name when you contact the other people. If your company offers an incentive for referrals, discuss this inducement for providing names.]

"I'd like to send you our newsletter (updates, specials) on a periodic basis just so you will be aware of what we're offering. Is email OK?" [Wait for the response. Confirm their email address or determine which one to use. You can also send them your contact information or vCard and send them a link to your website and blog, if you have one.]

[Discuss your next contact and agree on when and where that is to be and if it's by email, phone, or in-person. You might set a time to get together for breakfast or coffee depending on how close your offices are to each other.]

"I'll talk to (see) you again then. It's been really great

talking to you again. Appreciate the call and your help. Good-bye."

LATER WOULD BE BETTER — *"That's fine. It can wait."* [Set up a convenient time to talk again.]

"Talk to you then. Good-bye."

Call To An Old Contact

Use this scenario to call and talk with someone you know from your past well enough to speak to each other and have a conversation when you meet — but it's been a long time since you saw or spoke to each other. You want to make sure they know what your current role is, and you want to determine their interest level in what you are offering as well as enlist their help in identifying people that they know that might be interested in looking at or purchasing what you offer.

———

"Hi, <first name or nickname of your friend>, this is <your name>."

"How have you been? It's been a long time." [Wait for response.]

"We haven't talked in a while so I wanted to make sure that you knew that I am (began) working with <name of your company> (started my own business) and we're

located at <a general description or your location or service area is probably enough>."

"I wanted to say hello since it's been a while since we talked, but the main reason for my call is that I'd like your help. Do you have a moment now or would it be better for me to call back at a better time?" [Wait for response.]

Now Is OK — *"Fine."* [Talk about your business briefly so that they have a frame of reference. Listen for any interest they show.]

"I thought maybe you (your company) might have an interest in what we (I) offer or that you could help me identify people who might be interested in looking for a <term, name, or description of your product or service> in my area — now or in the near future. Possibly some people that you know that I don't."

[Listen for their general willingness to help you. If he or she mentions that they might have an interest or that they would like to help you, set up another call at a mutually convenient time.]

[If there seems to be no interest in what you offer or in helping you locate people who might have an interest in what you offer — or in establishing a strategic relationship — thank them, and change the subject or conclude the call.]

"Who are the first couple of names that come to mind right now that you think would take my call to let them know about what we do?" [Wait for response.]

[If they volunteer a name or two, write it down and ask for a way to contact that person or persons. Be sure to note the correct spelling and pronunciation. Get first names so you don't sound like a telemarketer or solicitor when you call them, and get permission to use their name when you contact the other people. If your company offers an incentive for referrals, discuss this inducement for providing names.]

"I'd like to send you our newsletter (updates, specials) on a periodic basis just so you will be aware of what we're offering. Is email OK?"

[Wait for the response. Confirm their email address or determine which one to use. You can also send them your contact information or vCard and send them a link to your website and blog, if you have one.]

[Discuss your next contact and agree on when and where that is to be and if it's by email, phone, or in-person. You can set a time to re-establish your relationship by getting together for coffee depending on how close your offices are to each other.]

"I'll talk to (see) you then. Really great talking to you again. Thanks for your help. Good-bye."

Now Is Not a Good Time — *"I knew that you might be busy and that you weren't expecting my call right now, but I thought I'd take a chance. Let me call back when you have a minute."* [Set up a convenient time to talk again.] *"Talk to you then. Good-bye."*

Later Would Be Better — *"That's fine. It can wait."* [Set up a convenient time to talk again.]

"Talk to you then. Good-bye."

Call From An Old Contact

Use this scenario when you get an unexpected call from someone you know from your past well enough to speak to each other and have a conversation when you meet — but it's been a long time since you spoke or saw each other. During this call, you want to make sure they know what your current role is, you want to get an idea of whether there might be any interest in what you offer, and you want to enlist their help in identifying people that they know that might be interested in looking at or purchasing what you offer.

———

[Answer the phone. Hear the other person identify themselves — unless you recognize their voice or your phone displays their name.] *"Hi, <first name or nickname of your friend>. Boy, it's been a while. Great to hear from you."*

[Listen to them and discuss what they want to talk with you about — after all, they are initiating the call. Then at an appropriate moment, if there is one, change gears and use the conversation to talk about what you want. If they can't stay on the call, or the reason for the call or the tone of the conversation doesn't seem appropriate for you to get into a business discussion, tell them you will call them back later to talk some more.]

[Address their issues, then transition into yours.]

"*I am so glad you called because I wanted to talk with you anyway. I recently began working with <name of your company> (just/recently started my own business) and we're located at <a general description is probably enough>.*" [Talk briefly about what you offer.]

[Listen for their general willingness to help you. If he or she mentions that they might have an interest or that they would like to help you, set up another call at a mutually convenient time.]

[If there seems to be no interest in what you offer or in helping you locate people who might have an interest in what you offer — or in establishing a strategic relationship — change the subject or conclude the call.]

"*You know, I could really use your help. Do you have another minute now or would it be better for me to give you a call later?*" [Wait for response.]

Now Is OK — *"Fine. I thought maybe you (your company) might have an interest in what we offer or that you could help me identify people who might be interested in looking for a <term, name, or description of your product or service> in my area — now or in the near future. Possibly some people that you know that I don't."*

[Listen for their general willingness to help you. If he or she mentions that they might have an interest or that they would like to help you, set up another call at a mutually convenient time.]

[If there seems to be no interest in what you offer or in helping you locate people who might have an interest in what you offer — or in establishing a strategic relationship — thank them, and change the subject or conclude the call.]

"Who are the first couple of names that come to mind right now that you think would take my call to let them know about what we do?" [Wait for response.]

[If they volunteer a name or two, write it down and ask for a way to contact that person or persons. Be sure to note the correct spelling and pronunciation. Get first names so you don't sound like a telemarketer or solicitor when you call them, and get permission to use their name when you contact the other people. If your company offers an incentive for referrals, discuss this inducement for providing names.]

"I'd like to send you our newsletter (updates, specials) on a periodic basis just so you will be aware of what we're offering. Is email OK?' [Wait for the response. Confirm their email address or determine which one to use. You can also send them your contact information or vCard and send them a link to your website and blog, if you have one.]

[Discuss your next contact and agree on when and where that is to be and if it's by email, phone, or in-person. You might set a time to get together for coffee depending on how close your offices are to each other.]

"I'll talk to (see) you again then. Really great hearing from you. Thanks for the call and your help. Good-bye."

LATER WOULD BE BETTER — *"That's fine. It can wait."* [Set up a convenient time to talk again.] *"Talk to you then. Good-bye."*

Call To A Professional Friend

Use this scenario to call and talk with a professional friend of yours. Depending on the nature of your business or your circle of contacts, it could be builder, Realtor®, contractor, architect, attorney, appraiser, consultant, banker, professor, accountant, physician, or other type of professional or business owner. You want to make sure they know what your current role is, determine if they have any potential interest in what you offer, and you want to enlist their help in identifying people that they know that might be interested in looking at or purchasing what you offer.

———

"Hi, <first name or nickname of your friend>."

"I wanted to make sure that you're aware that I recently began working with <name of your company> (just/recently started my own business) and we're located at <a general description is probably enough>." [Mention very briefly what you do, such as your major product or service or chief mission.]

"You know, I could really use your help. Do you have another minute now or would it be better for me to give you a call later?' [Wait for response.]

Now Is OK — *"Fine. I thought maybe you (your company) might have an interest in what we (I) offer that we could discuss at another time or that you could help me identify people who might be interested in looking for a <term, name, or description of your product or service> in my area (your area) — now or in the near future. Possibly some people that you know that I don't."*

[Listen for their general willingness to help you. If he or she mentions that they might have an interest or that they would like to help you, set up another call at a mutually convenient time.]

[If there seems to be no interest in what you offer or in helping you locate people who might have an interest in what you offer — or in establishing a strategic relationship — thank them, and change the subject or conclude the call.]

"*Who are the first couple of names that come to mind right now that you think would take my call to let them know about what we do?*" [Wait for response.]

[If they volunteer a name or two, write it down and ask for a way to contact that person or persons. Be sure to note the correct spelling and pronunciation. Get first names so you don't sound like a telemarketer or solicitor when you call them, and get permission to use their name when you contact the other people. Be sensitive to the fact that some professionals may not want their name used or that they would like to be the one to make the introduction to you. If your company offers an incentive for referrals, discuss this inducement for providing names.]

"*I'd like to send you our newsletter (updates, specials) on a periodic basis just so you will be aware of what we're offering. Is email OK?*" [Wait for the response. Confirm their email address or determine which one to use. You can also send them your contact information or vCard and send them a link to your website and blog, if you have one.]

[Discuss your next contact and agree on when and where that is to be and if it's by email, phone, or in-person. You might set a time to get together for coffee depending on how close your offices are to each other.]

"I'll talk to (see) you again then. Really great hearing from you. Thanks for the call and your help. Good-bye."

LATER WOULD BE BETTER — *"That's fine. It can wait."* [Set up a convenient time to talk again.] *"Talk to you then. Good-bye."*

Call To A New Purchaser

Use this scenario to call and talk with someone who has purchased something from you recently — even if they purchased hasn't been delivered, installed, or completed yet. You want to help keep them excited about their decision and request their help in identifying people that they know that you can contact about what you offer.

––––––

"Hi, <first name or nickname of your consumer>."

[Thank them again for their purchase, answer any questions or concerns that they mention, complete your small talk, and then get to the reason for your call.]

"We are (I am) really excited about your decision to own one of our <name or description of your product> (have us conduct/complete type or description of service or installation>) and appreciate you selecting to do business with us. I am sure that you (you guys) are (you're) excited as well about your new <name or description or product or service>." [Wait for response.]

"You've probably had a chance to think of several of your friends, colleagues, or associate [depending on what you offer] *that you feel should at least look at or consider what we offer to see if some of them would benefit from what we do as well."* [Wait for response.]

"Who are the first two or three people who come to mind that you think really ought to look at what we have to offer?" [Wait for a response and be prepared to write down any names they give you and ask for a way to contact the friends that they tell you about. Be sure to note the correct spelling and pronunciation. Get first names so you don't sound like a telemarketer or solicitor. Get permission to use your purchaser's name(s) when you contact the other people. If your company offers an incentive program for referrals — maybe just for new purchasers, discuss this with them.]

They Have Names to Give You — *"That's great. I'll invite them to look at what we have to offer, and I'll let you know what happened. Can you think of anyone else?"* [Wait for response.]

"Thanks for your help. I really appreciate it."

"We're really looking forward to having you as one of our satisfied customers, and we appreciate you choosing us to provide <name or description of your product or service> for you."

"Please let me know if there's anything I can do for you. Good-bye."

No Names to Give You at This Time — *"That's quite all right. You'll probably think of some later on, and you can tell me about them the next time we talk or you can text or email them to me. Then I'll contact them and discuss what they're looking for and how we can help them."*

"We're really looking forward to having you as one of our satisfied customers, and we appreciate you choosing us to provide <name or description of your product or service> for you."

"Please let me know if there's anything I can do for you. Good-bye."

Call To A Recent Purchaser

Use this scenario to call and talk with someone who has purchased something from you within the past 6 months that you're sure is satisfied with your relationship. You want to use their pleasant experience to request their help in identifying people that they know that you can contact about what you offer.

———

"Hi, <first name or nickname of your consumer>."

[Thank them again for their purchase and their satisfaction, complete your small talk, and then get to the reason for your call.] *"I'm honored to have been able to work with you (I'm so happy that you chose to work with us, It has been a real pleasure working with you and getting to know you) and so happy that you are enjoying your <name of product or service they purchased from you> (you have enjoyed working with us, too)."*

"As you've been using your <name of product or service they purchased from you>, you've probably had a chance to think of several of your friends or associates that you think should know about it as well and have a chance to decide if they would like to enjoy it also." [Wait for response.]

"Who are the first two or three people who come to mind that you think really ought to look at what we have to offer?" [Wait for a response and be prepared to write down any names they give you and ask for a way to contact the friends that they tell you about. Be sure to note the correct spelling and pronunciation. Get first

names so you don't sound like a telemarketer or solicitor. Get permission to use your purchaser's names when you contact the other people. If your company offers an incentive program for referrals — maybe just for new purchasers or with certain other qualifications, discuss this with them.]

They Have Names to Give You — *"That's great. I'll contact them and find out how I think we can help them, too — and then I'll let you know what happened. Can you think of anyone else?"* [Wait for response.]

"Thanks for your help. I really appreciate it. Please let me know if there's anything I can do for you. Good-bye."

No Names to Give You at This Time — *"That's quite all right. You'll probably think of some later on, and you can tell me about them the next time we talk or you can email them to me. Then I'll contact them and see how I might be able to help them as well."*

"Please let me know if there's anything I can do for you. Good-bye."

Call To Existing Customer

Use this scenario to call and talk with people who have been using your product or service for more than 6 months to request their help in identifying people that they know that you can contact about what you offer since they have had a great experience with your product or service — and you.

———

"*Hi, <first name or nickname of your consumer>.*" [Sincerely thank them for being a satisfied customer, complete your small talk, and then get to the reason for your call.]

"*I'm honored to have been able to work with you (I'm so happy that you chose to work with us, It has been a real pleasure working with you and getting to know you) and so happy that you are enjoying your <name of product or service they purchased from you> (you have enjoyed working with us, too).*"

"*I'd like your help for a minute. As you've been enjoying your <name of product or service they purchased from you>, I imagine you've probably had a chance to think of several of your friends or associates that you think should know about it as well and have a chance to decide if they would like to enjoy it also.*" [Wait for response.]

"*Who are the first two or three people who come to mind that you think really ought to look at what we have to offer?*" [Wait for a response. Be prepared to write down any names they give you and ask for a way to contact them. Be sure to note the correct spelling and pronunciation. Get first names so you don't sound like a telemarketer or solicitor. Get permission to use your homeowner's name(s) when you contact the other people. If your company offers an incentive program for referrals, discuss this with them.]

They Have Names to Give You — *"That's great. I'll contact them and find out how I think we can help them, too — and then I'll let you know what happened. Can you think of anyone else?"* [Wait for response.]

"Thanks for your help. I really appreciate it. Please let me know if there's anything I can do for you. Good-bye."

No Names to Give You at This Time — *"That's quite all right. You'll probably think of some later on, and you can tell me about them the next time we talk or you can email them to me. Then I'll invite them to visit us and take a look at our homes."*

"Please let me know if there's anything I can do for you. Good-bye."

Call Back To Your Regular Service & Repair People

Use this scenario to call and talk with people that you see on a regular basis who provide technical and repair services and help maintain your office and equipment. This would be a call between their regular visits — after you talked with them and made the request for help in-person and they said to check back with them. You want their help in identifying people that they know that you can contact about what you offer.

———

"Hi, <first name or nickname of your service provider>."

[Complete your small talk, and then get to the reason for your call.] *"When we spoke the last time you were here, I asked you who you might know or might have heard of in your travels who is in the market for what I (we) provide that should take a look at what we have to offer, and you told me that you needed some time to think of someone. I was wondering who you have thought of that should take a look at what we have?"* [Wait for response.]

[If he or she readily volunteers a name or two now, write it down and ask for a way to contact them. Be sure to note the correct spelling and pronunciation. Get first names so you don't sound like a telemarketer or solicitor, and get permission to use the person's name that is giving you the referrals when you contact the other people.]

They Have Names to Give You — *"That's great. I will call them and discuss what we offer and see if there is any interest. The next time you drop by I'll let you know what happened. Can you think of anyone else?"* [Wait for response.]

"Thanks. I appreciate your help. See you next time (or specific day if it's soon). Have a great day."

"By the way, have you passed out any of the business cards I gave you?" [Wait for response and discuss the circumstances if that if it has happened.] *"Thanks again. Good-bye."*

No Names to Give You at This Time — *"That's quite all right. Thanks for trying."*

"Again, if anyone comes to mind that you think should know about what I (we) offer, you can tell them about what we're doing, or you can let me know who they are whenever you come in and I'll give them a call to see if they have any interest."

"I really appreciate your help. See you again next time. By the way, have you passed out any of the business cards I gave you?" [Wait for response and discuss the circumstances if that if it has happened.]

"Have a good one. Good-bye."

Asking For A Referral On An Incoming Phone Inquiry

Use this scenario after talking with someone who called in for information about what you offer when you learn that they do not appear to like or want what you provide — ask for their help in identifying other people who might be interested your products or services.

———

"I appreciate your call and your initial interest. I'm sorry that you don't think we can meet your needs from what we've just briefly discussed, but I'm just curious. You must have thought we were worth checking out or you wouldn't have called, so let me ask you this."

"Who can you think of who might be in a similar situation as you that you think might like to hear about or look at (consider) what we have to offer? I'd be happy to contact them and see if they would be interested in what we have to offer." [Wait for response.]

[If they volunteer a name or two, write it down and ask for a way to contact that person or persons. Be sure to note the correct spelling and pronunciation. Get first names so you don't sound like a telemarketer or solicitor, and get permission to use the person's name that is giving you the referrals when you contact the names they are giving you. Determine the best form of contact for the people who are being referred to you.]

They Have Names to Give You — *"That's great. Can you think of anyone else?"* [Wait for response.] *"Thanks for your help. I really appreciate it."*

"Thanks for contacting us, and good luck finding what you need. Good-bye."

No Names to Give You at This Time — *"That's quite all right. Thanks for trying and thanks for your interest in our company (what we offer). Good-bye."*

Post-Visit Call To Ask For A Referral

Use this scenario to call someone after an initial presentation — regardless of where this occurs — as part of a planned contact or as a special call just to ask for their help in identifying other people who might be interested in what you offer.

––––––

"Hello <use their first name — even use their nickname if they indicated one when you met them>? This is <your name> from <name of your company>."

"I really enjoyed getting to meet you and being able to tell you a little bit about who we are and what we provide."

"Now that you've had a chance to see what we're all about, maybe you've thought of some people who ought to see for themselves what we offer. Who are the first two names (Who is the first person) that come to mind that I should call or email to let them know about what we offer?" [Wait for response.]

[Be prepared to write down any names they give you and ask for a way to contact those people. Be sure to note the correct spelling and pronunciation. Get first names so you don't sound like a telemarketer or solicitor. Get permission to use your resident's names when you contact the other people. If your company offers an incentive to customers for referrals, discuss this inducement for providing names.]

They Have Names to Give You — *"That's great. I'll contact them and find out if they have any interest in learning more about how we can help them. Then I'll let you know what they said. Can you think of anyone else?"* [Wait for response.]

"Thanks for your help. I really appreciate it. Good-bye."

No Names to Give You at This Time — *"That's quite all right. Thanks for trying. Maybe the name of someone will come to you later that you can pass along to me."*

"I'd like to send you our newsletter (specials, coupons) periodically just so you will be aware of what we're offering. Is email OK?" [Wait for the response. Confirm their email address or determine which one to use. You can also talk about or send them a link to your blog if you have one.]

"Fine. I'll call you again in a week (two weeks, month) to make sure that you have received what I have sent you."

"If you happen to think of anyone between now and when we talk again who might be interested in the opportunities we offer here at <name of your company>, you can tell me about them at that time."

"Again, thanks for your help (interest), and let me know if there's anything I can do for you. Good-bye."

Post-Visit Call To Ask For
Additional Referrals

Use this scenario as another reason to call someone that you've already met and talked with about what you offer — who has already given you the name of someone that you could contact — to thank them for their help already, to pursue the sale with them, and to request additional referrals.

———

"Hello <use their first name — even use their nickname if they indicated one when you met them>? This is <your name> from <name of your company>."

"When we met (spoke) the other day (a specific day), you gave me the name of <state the name or names of the people who were provided> as being in the market for <name or description of the product or type of services you provide> that we have to offer here at <your company>. I really appreciate you sharing their name (these names) with me, and I wanted to let you

know that I called them and <report generally on what happened when you contacted these people>."

"I was wondering if you had been able to think of any other people who might have an interest in our product (products, services)." [Wait for response.]

They Have More Names to Give You — *"Great. Who are they?"* [Wait for response.]

[Be prepared to write down any names they give you and ask for a way to contact those people. Be sure to note the correct spelling and pronunciation. Get first names so you don't sound like a telemarketer or solicitor. Get permission to use their name(s) when you contact the other people.]

"I'll contact these people just as I did the others that you gave to me, and I will call you back to let you know what happens. Thanks again for your help. Good-bye."

No Names to Give You at This Time — *"That's quite all right. I appreciate your help."*

"By the way, I'd like to take you to breakfast next week (whenever our schedules allow within the next couple of weeks) to show my appreciation for your help." [Wait for response and agree upon a day, time, and location if they accept your invitation.]

"Would you like for me to call you or email you a reminder?" [Wait for response.]

Yes — *"Fine. I'll email (call, text) you on <mention the specific day> to remind you of our appointment on <day, time, and location>. Which do you prefer?"* [Wait for response. Confirm the email address or phone number they want you to use, or write it down as you obtain it.]

"I look forward to seeing you then. Good-bye."

No — *"Fine. I'll plan on seeing you then on <mention the day and time> at <place>. Good-bye."*

Second Call To Ask For A Referral

Use this scenario to call someone that you talked with about what you offer who was unable to think of or provide you with any referrals for you to contact during your initial meeting or last telephone conversation with them — this time to ask them again for any names they can furnish. This might be someone from your circle of contacts or a person you have met as you are doing your presentations.

———

"Hello <use their first name — even use their nickname if they indicated one>? This is <your name> from <name of your company>."

"When we met (spoke) the other day (the last time, <a specific day>), I asked who you knew that might be interested in what we offer, and you weren't able to think of anyone. I thought that maybe since then that you'd thought of one or two people that should know about what we are offering (what we provide)."

"Who comes to mind now that you think I should call and talk to (email) about what we offer to see if they might have any interest in learning more about how we can help them?" [Wait for response.]

No Names to Give You at This Time — *"I understand, and I appreciate your help and taking time to talk with me again."*

"I'd like to send you our newsletter (specials, coupons) on a periodic basis just so you'll be aware of what we're offering. Is email OK?"

[Wait for response. Confirm their email address or determine which one to use. You can also talk about or send them a link to your blog if you have one.]

"I'll check back with you in a few weeks to make sure you're getting the newsletter, and if anyone comes to mind that you think should know about what we do (our products, our services), you can tell me then."

"Good talking with you again. Good-bye."

They Have Names to Give You — *"Great. Who are they?"*

[Wait for response. Write down any names they give you and ask for a way to contact those people. Be sure to note the correct spelling and pronunciation. Get first names so you don't sound like a telemarketer or solicitor. Get permission to use their name when you contact the other people.]

"I'll call them and discuss who we are and what we offer here at <name of your company> to see if they have any interest in learning more about how we can help them. Then I'll call you after I have spoken with them to let you know what happened."

"Good talking with you again. Thanks for your help. I really appreciate it. Good-bye."

Leaving A Voice Message After A Brief Initial Meeting

Use this scenario for someone you've recently met when you get the person's voice mail when you call. Be prepared to leave a voice mail message, but only leave the following message — and only do it on the initial call. After that, no messages regardless of how many times you call and reach the machine. Just hang up before the tone.

———

"Hi, <their first name>. This is <your complete name, first and last> of <your company>."

"I met you briefly last night (the other day, Tuesday, last Wednesday, over the weekend) at (mention the specific event or place where you met, such as chamber of commerce breakfast, church, jury duty, Little League game, the mall, a specific store or restaurant, the Rotary Club, PTA, planning committee, etc.) — basically just long enough for us to exchange business cards." [Be sure to mention the place or the circumstances for the meeting.]

"I was calling to say hello again and see if we could set up a time to talk for a few minutes over coffee to learn more about each other's business."

"I possibly could use your help."

"I'm sorry I missed you. I'll try again another time, but my number here is <telephone number>."

"Thanks. I look forward to talking with you again soon."

[If they call back, that's great. Be prepared to have a conversation with them just as if you had reached them successfully when you telephoned originally.]

6

Reaching Out In Writing

The Value Of Writing

In addition to using personal and telephone communication with people that you already know, sometimes it might be easier or more convenient to reach out to them with a letter, email, or text message.

It isn't always quicker or as effective as talking to someone in person or by telephone, but you can do it according to your schedule and not be concerned whether the person you are connecting with is available at that particular moment to receive your message.

Using a written message, such as email, card, or letter — or even an occasional text or instant message — is also useful for documenting your requests and for passing along your contact information.

When you need to include a postcard, your business card, or a survey, written communication is the best form of contact to use.

Letters work well also when it's been a long time since you have talked to your friend or customer. They help re-establish your relationship. Then you can follow with a phone call or email.

Using Email

While email is not appropriate for working with people that you don't know because it's less formal and their spam filter may not allow your message to get through, it's fine to use emails for communicating with friends and others that you know.

When you send emails, your email address and your company website address (URL) should be **active links** so that the person you're contacting can reply back or go to your website without entering any information.

They can just hit the link ("'control' + 'click'") and go right to a reply screen with your email address already filled in, or they can go directly to your website homepage.

Also, go for a consistent look in your email address. Don't use "yourname@gmail.com" address part of the time and "yourname@yourcompany.com" at other times.

Even though you are communicating with friends, do not use a personal-looking email address unless you are such good friends that they will easily recognize it.

Most of the time, addresses such as "fredlikesfishing@," "packersfan@," or "mary1267@" are too casual for business communication.

If you don't have an email at your corporate domain name — or choose not to use it since your friends may not recognize it — go with a gmail, outlook, or yahoo email address.

Getting Email Delivered

You want the person who receives your email message to open it and read it, so avoid anything that might keep it from getting into their inbox.

If you're not sure how their email client accepts attachments, it's best not to include them and to put them in the body of your email. Keep them very short.

People worry about viruses, and some email programs could reject your message, or send it to the junk folder.

In your subject line, avoid anything cutesy or vague. Putting the name of your company or anything to do with sales may get flagged. Just include your own name, such as *"Message/Hello from Steve Hoffacker."*

Familiarity Helps

Unlike contacting strangers where a certain amount of formality and propriety are important, connecting with your friends and people you know can be more casual and spontaneous.

Messages can be brief and can include more personal references. You can ask about them and their family or recall a common activity, for instance.

Don't be sloppy — you are still conducting business. However, phrases, some slang, and even humor can be used to help it sound more conversational with your friends. Avoid anything off-color.

Email is never advisable for an initial introduction to someone you are attempting to establish a relationship with but is fine to use with people you know. Just make sure you have a current email address before reaching out to them.

Texting And Instant Messaging

Text messaging ("texting") may be a good way to contact some of your closest friends and relatives — especially if you have texted them previously about others matters or know that they like to communicate this way. Perhaps they have texted you previously. It can be a good change of pace for contact.

Nevertheless, texting should never be done to introduce yourself to someone you have not met and should only be used when you know the person well enough for them to appreciate that you contacted them in this way and for them to respond to your text.

Even social networking sites like Facebook and Twitter can be great resources for leaving messages and communicating with your friends and network.

Using "chat" on Facebook or instant messaging on other sites — when you notice friends and acquaintances online — is an excellent way to initiate or maintain contact with them.

Writing Requires Minimal Effort

In this chapter, I've assembled some examples of letters, cards, and emails (and a couple of text messages) that you can use as you contact people that you do business with, those you have met socially or at business functions, ones you see occasionally, friends that you see often or rarely, distant family members, people you have sold to or talked with during a presentation, professionals whose services you use, or others that you want to communicate with in writing about what you are doing and how you can use their help.

Remember the reason you use the letter, card, or email is to communicate when an in-person or verbal approach is not practical or necessary. Having your message delivered must happen before it can be read.

Use these suggested letters, cards and emails exactly as they are or modify them for your writing style, personality, and degree of formality.

Intentionally, the suggested letters are a little more formal, printed cards a little so, and notecards fairly short and informal since they are handwritten. The suggested emails are in a relatively informal email style with more paragraphs that a letter.

Writing Is Only One Approach

Remember that the reason you are using the letter, card, email, or even in a few cases a text message, is to communicate to people you already know when you do not need to actually be speaking directly to them by phone or in-person — or when reaching them by phone or seeing them in-person is not easily done.

In some cases, this approach might be sufficient. In others, this will be a prelude to a phone conversation or meeting.

Use these suggested letters, cards, and emails exactly as they are or modify them for your writing style.

They should not have a strong sales message.

The main thing your communication is doing is letting your circle of contacts know what you do so you can talk with about what you offer and also request their help.

Your Signature Block

In the interest of keeping the following examples of letters as short as possible — showing just the salutation and main body of the message or letter — the following information (even if you already have mentioned it elsewhere in the body of the letter, such as your phone number, email address, or website) should be added after the text provided as a way of closing the letter, email, or note:

Sincerely,
<space>
<Company name>
<space>
<Your signature> (digital for emails)
<space>
<Your name — as you want your customers to call you — plus any professional designations>
<Your position or title>
<Your direct phone line or extension>
<Your fax number>
<Your cell phone number>
<Your email address> (linked in emails)
<Your company website> (linked in emails)

<Your company blog address> (linked in emails)
<space>
<Your company or brand "tagline">
<space>
<Your social media widgets> (linked in emails)
<space>
<Any attachments or enclosures>

Signing Cards

For notecards and postcards — especially ones that are handwritten or commercial greeting cards (that you buy at the store) — just sign them in your own hand. Don't use a stamp or electronic signature.

Using just your first name is fine — especially if you know them very well. For others that you know but aren't sure if they will recognize you by just your first name because they likely know several people with your same first name or you haven't talked with in a while, you might want to use your complete name.

You don't need to sign your name with your professional designations or title. That will be on your business card that you are enclosing.

Be sure to enclose a business card in the envelope along with the note or place it inside the greeting card (obviously this can't be done with a postcard) to supply the other contact information — even if some of your contact information is printed elsewhere on the card. For emails, include hot (active) links to your email address, website, blog, social media profiles, and any references that you include. Be sure to test them to make sure they work before sending the email.

The Inside Address

Unlike a letter to someone that you haven't met before, most of your letters to your circle of contacts will be less formal. As such, they won't require an inside address.

When you are sending a letter to someone you just met as the first step in developing the relationship, you may want to use a customary inside address with:

<Name, including any professional designations> or
<Names, if a couple>
<Title or Position, if applicable>
<Name of Business, if sent to the business>
<Business Address, including department, suite number, floor, or building, if sent to the business>
<Home Address, including apartment number, if sent to the residence>
<City, State, Zip>

For notes, cards, emails, and text messages — and for the majority of your letters — the inside address would not be used.

It's a good idea to put the date at the top of any letter, card, or note that you are sending — even if there is no inside address.

Letter After A Brief Introduction

Use this letter — typically written on your computer and printed out although it can be handwritten if you like — after meeting someone briefly at a business or social function to acknowledge the meeting and set up a future telephone conversation with them. At that future meeting, you can enlist their help and pursue a business relationship with them. Keep this letter fairly brief and cordial — no sales message.

——————

<First name of new friend or acquaintance>,

I'm glad I had the opportunity (chance) to meet you last night (Tuesday, yesterday, recently) at <specific event or place where you met, such as seminar, mixer, reception, chamber of commerce breakfast, church, Little League game, youth soccer game, seminar, Rotary Club, etc.>. Unfortunately, we didn't get a chance to talk to each other very much. It seemed like we just met long enough to exchange business cards and that was about it.

I would like to learn more about your business and get a chance, as well, to tell you about what we are doing here at <name of your company>. I will give you a call in a couple of days to see when you are available to grab a cup of coffee so we can talk some more.

In the meantime, you may reach me at <telephone number> or email me at <email address>. You might also want to visit our website at <website address>.

I look forward to talking with you again.

Printed Notecard After
A Brief Introduction

Rather than a letter (handwritten or printed), you may choose to use a notecard, such a one imprinted with the name and logo of your company that you can print out with your message on your computer. Use this after meeting someone briefly at a business or social function to acknowledge the meeting and set up a future telephone conversation. At that future meeting, you can enlist their help and pursue a business relationship with them. Notes are typically brief and to the point — avoid a sales message or reference.

————

<First name of new friend or acquaintance>,

I'm glad I had the opportunity (chance) to meet you last night (Tuesday, yesterday, last week) at <specific event or place where you met, such as seminar, mixer,

reception, charity event, golf outing, home builders association or Realtor® association event, chamber of commerce breakfast, church, Little League game, youth soccer game, Rotary Club, committee meeting, etc.>.

I will give you a call in a couple of days to see when you are available for coffee so we can talk some more.

In the meantime, you may reach me at <telephone number> or email me at <email address>.

You might also want to visit our website at <address>.

I look forward to talking with you again.

Handwritten Notecard After A Brief Introduction

You may want to use a handwritten note on your company notecards rather than a computer printed message to contact someone you just met at a business or social function to set up a future telephone conversation. Just write as legibly as you can. You may want to print in all caps if your penmanship is not strong. At that future meeting, you can enlist their help and pursue a business relationship with them. You want your note to be cordial and fairly brief.

———

<First name of new friend or acquaintance>,

I'm glad we met last night (Tuesday, yesterday, last week) at <specific event or place where you met, such as seminar, mixer, reception, charity event, golf outing, home builders association or Realtor® association event, chamber of commerce breakfast, church, Little League game, youth soccer game, Rotary Club, committee meeting, etc.>.

I will give you a call in a couple of days to see when you are available for coffee so we can talk some more.

In the meantime, you may reach me at <telephone number> or email me at <email address>.

You might also want to visit our website at <website address>.

I look forward to talking with you again.

Handwritten Note In A Greeting Card After A Brief Introduction

You can choose to use a handwritten message inside a commercial greeting card (a card with a success message or one with an inspirational picture and message) rather than using a note or letter — just jot your message in the blank space above the fold or on the left side of the fold of the card to contact someone you just met at a business or social function to set up a future telephone conversation. At that future meeting, you can enlist their help and pursue a business relationship with them. You want your note to be cordial and very brief.

––––––

<First name of new friend or acquaintance>,

I'm glad we met last night (Tuesday, yesterday, last week) at <specific event or place where you met, such as seminar, mixer, reception, charity event, golf outing, home builders association or Realtor® association event, chamber breakfast, church, Little League game, youth soccer game, Rotary Club, committee meeting, etc.>.

I will give you a call in a couple of days to see when you are available for coffee so we can talk some more.

I enclosed my card with my contact information.

I look forward to talking with you again.

Email After A Brief Introduction

Email is a very acceptable and convenient way for businesspeople and friends to communicate today, so you may choose to use this rather than a letter, note, or card to contact someone you just met at a business or social function to set up a future telephone conversation. At that future meeting, you can enlist their help and pursue a business relationship with them. This is a fairly informal method of contact and should be used within 24 hours of the original meeting.

———

<First name of new friend or acquaintance>,

I'm glad I had the opportunity (chance) to meet you (I enjoyed meeting you) last night (this morning, yesterday, over the weekend, Wednesday morning, Monday night) at <specific event or place where you met, such as seminar, mixer, reception, chamber of commerce breakfast, church, Little League game, youth soccer game, Realtors® association, the mall, a specific store or restaurant, Rotary Club, etc.>.

I would like to learn more about your business and what you do. I'd also like to tell you a little about (talk about) what we are doing here at <name of your company>.

I'll give you a call in a couple of days (tomorrow, Tuesday, the first of the week, later in the week) to see when you are available to get (have, let me buy you) a cup of coffee.

If you like, you can contact me at <telephone number> or <email address> [linked].

You might also want to check out (take a look at, visit) our website at <website address> [linked]. [You can mention your blog or facebook page also.]

For easy reference, I have attached a copy of my vCard.

I look forward to talking with you again.

Letter To Friend Or Acquaintance

Use this letter on your company letterhead to notify friends and acquaintances of your new position and to lay the foundation for talking with them about what you do and for referrals. This is going to be a more casual and informal style of letter than most you would use. Keep it relatively short since you can visit with them later or use text, phone, or email to pursue your referral needs. Keep this letter strictly informational, as you don't want to appear that the only reason you are contacting them is for their help. Depending on your relationship with them, you can add a short personal note, such as asking about how something turned out or offering congratulations on some good news you heard about for them.

––––––

<First name of your friend or acquaintance>,

I don't know if you've heard or not, but I wanted to make sure you knew (are aware) that I am now representing <your company> (started my own business), located at <physical address>.

I'm excited about the opportunities and our direction.

For now, I just wanted to make sure you were aware of what I'm doing and that you have my current contact information.

I'll call you soon to see (discuss, talk about) when we can get together (have coffee, get a drink, grab lunch, have breakfast).

In the meantime, feel free to call me anytime on my cell phone at <number> or email me at <email address>.

Printed Notecard To A
Friend Or Acquaintance

Rather than a letter, you may choose to use an informal note or notecard card imprinted with the name and logo of your company that you print out on your computer to notify friends and acquaintances of your new position and to lay the foundation for potential future business and referrals. The note format is good because you want to keep it relatively short anyway since you can visit with them later or text, phone, or email them to pursue your referral needs. Keep this note strictly informational — you don't want it to appear that you are contacting them just for their help.

———

<First name of your friend or acquaintance>,

I wanted to make sure you are aware (know) that I just/recently started representing <name of your company> (just started/opened my own company/ business) located at <physical address>. (I've changed companies since we last spoke, and now I'm <title of position> here at <name of your company> in <name of area or physical location>.)

I just started (I've been here just <approximate length of time in weeks or months>) (I've/we've been open about < approximate length of time in weeks or months>).

I'll call you soon to give you some more details and see when we can get together for a cup of coffee (breakfast, lunch).

For now, I just wanted to make sure you were aware of what I'm doing and that you have my current contact information.

In the meantime, feel free to call me anytime on my cell phone at <number> or email me at <email address>.

Handwritten Notecard To A Friend Or Acquaintance

Use this personal handwritten notecard on your official company notepaper or notecard to notify your friends and acquaintances of your current status and to lay the foundation for potential future business and referrals.

Keep this note strictly informational, as you don't want to appear that you are contacting them just for their help. You may want to print in all caps rather than use cursive.

———

<First name of your friend or acquaintance>,

I wanted to make sure that you're aware that I just started representing <name of your company> (just started/opened my own company/business) located at <physical address or service area>.

I've just been here/open <approximate length of time>.

I'll call you soon to give you some more details and see when we can get together for a cup of coffee (breakfast, lunch, a drink).

I just wanted to make sure you were aware of what I'm doing and that you have my current contact information.

Email To A Friend Or Acquaintance On Your New Position

Email is a convenient way to communicate with friends and acquaintances when you have their current email address. This informal message is a great way to let people know what you are doing and to lay the foundation for potential future business and referrals. It should remain primarily informational, but there can be some personal references also because of the format. Just don't make it seem that you are contacting them just for their help or trying to make a sale.

———

<First name of your friend or acquaintance>,

Just a quick note to let you know that I've relocated (moved, changed) from my last position. I wasn't sure if you knew about this so I wanted to make sure I told you that I recently started here as <title of position> at <name of your company> (just started/opened my own company/ business), located at <physical address or landmark>.

I've attached a vCard with my new contact information.

I'm excited about the opportunities and our direction, and I'll call you soon to see (discuss, talk about) when we can get together.

In the meantime, feel free to give me a call on my cell at <cell number> or email me at <email address> [linked].

Talk to you soon.

Email To A Friend Or Acquaintance For A Referral

After you have re-established contact with your close circle of contacts, email is a great way to reach out to them to request the names of people for you to contact that might be interested in what you offer.

———

<First name of your friend or acquaintance>,

When we last spoke (talked) I told you about what we are doing here at <name of your company>, and I mentioned that I could use your help in identifying people that might be looking for what we offer (a new <name or description of product you carry>).

Has anyone come to mind that I could talk to?

I just want them to see for themselves if what we offer interests them. If it does, great. If not, that's OK, too.

Let me know who I should be talking to, and then let them know that I will contacting them.

Thanks for your help.

Text Message To A Friend, Relative, Or Acquaintance For Update

Use this brief text message to contact someone you know well enough to communicate with them in this way (relative, close friend, or acquaintance) to let them know of your new position and to set up another contact by phone or have an email or text mail exchange with them. For purposes of this template, abbreviations that often are used in texting will not be used. However, if you have already been texting this person and typically type all in lower case or use shorthand or abbreviations, then using "4" for "for," "cn u" for "can you," "ur" for "your," "u" for "you," "BTW" for "by the way" and other such notations or styling would be fine to use. Otherwise, avoid them and keep it businesslike.

―――――

<Their first name>, I just started selling <name of product or service> here at <name of your company> (recently opened/began my own business) in <general location>. Would love to catch up with you over coffee. What's your schedule (What's convenient for you)? <Your first name>

Text Message To A Friend, Relative, Or Acquaintance For Referral

Use this brief text message to contact someone you know well enough to communicate with them in this way (relative, friend, or acquaintance). You want to find out who they know that might have an interest in using what you offer that they can refer to you. Again, if you have already been texting this person and typically use shorthand notations, it's fine to continue doing that. Otherwise, keep it businesslike.

―――――

<Their first name>, I can use your help. I think I told you that I am selling <name or description of product or service> in <name of your area> with <name of your company> (for myself). I would appreciate hearing about anyone that you know who might be looking for a new <type or name of product or service> in my area in the near future. Any ideas? Thanks. <Your first name>

Email To A Social Networking Contact

Use this email message to contact any person that you know through social networking sites that you have blogged with or connected with online. You mainly want to talk with them by phone or have an email exchange — rather than set a meeting — to determine if they (or their company) have any interest in what you offer (based on what business they are in or what you know about them through their profile and postings) or who they know who might have an interest in what you offer that they can refer to you.

———

<Their first name>, [If you're contacting them through the social networking site and using the email platform there, there won't be a need for establishing how you know each other. Otherwise, an opening line reminding them of how you know each other might be necessary.]

You may have noticed, but In case you weren't aware of what I do, I sell <name or description of products or

services> in <name of your area or town> with <name of your company> (for myself).

I thought maybe you could help me. I am looking for people, possibly even you or your company, who might be interested in a <name, description, or type of product or service you offer> — now or in the near future.

If you have any ideas, I would appreciate hearing about them. If you can't think of anyone, that's OK. Maybe later.

Thanks for your help.

Email To A Professional Contact

Email is a convenient way to reach out to professionals in your area that you know to let them know about your new position or endeavor and to lay the foundation for potential future business (depending on what you offer and the nature of their business) and for referrals from their circle of contacts.

<First name of your friend or colleague>,

Just a quick note to let you know that I've relocated (moved) from my last position (started/opened my own business/practice). I wasn't sure if you knew about this so I wanted to make sure I told you that I'm with <name

of your company> (on my own), and we're located at <physical address or landmark>.

I'm excited about the opportunities and direction here.

I'll give you a call soon to talk more about what we have and how it might work out for you or some of your customers (clients, friends).

In the meantime, feel free to give me a call on my cell at <cell number> or email me at <email address> [linked]. I've attached a vCard with my new contact information.

Talk to you soon.

Letter To A New Purchaser

Use this letter that you generate on your computer to contact someone who has purchased a product or service from you recently — even if it hasn't been delivered, installed, or completed. Your letter thanks them for doing business with you and requests their help in identifying people who should know about what you offer.

———

<First name or names of your new purchaser>,

Thank you for the confidence you have placed in me and my (our) company by choosing to do business with us (ordering our <name or description of product or service>).

I trust you are still as excited about your decision as you were the day you made it. I imagine also that you probably have several friends, family members, and co-workers show an interest in what you have selected.

I would love to talk with (show) anyone that you think should know about what we offer how they could benefit as well.

I have enclosed a stamped, addressed postcard for you to jot down the names and contact information for a couple of people that you think should know about what we offer or have specifically asked about what you have selected so I can contact them and give them a little more information on what we do. If you prefer, you can email it to me at <email address>.

Thanks for your help. If there's anything I can do for you, please let me know.

[If they haven't received the item they purchased from you, comment about the anticipated delivery or completion date.]

Printed Notecard To
A New Purchaser

Rather than a letter, you may choose to use a notecard imprinted with the name and logo of your company that you print out on your computer to contact a new purchaser. It's less formal than a letter. This note is used to thank them for their business and to ask for referrals.

———

<First name or names of your new purchaser>,

Thank you for your trust (confidence) in selecting us for your <name or description of product or service>.

As you are enjoying (getting ready to start using, waiting on delivery/installation/completion of) your new <name or description of product or service>, I imagine that you probably have thought of several friends, associates, family members, and co-workers who might like to have one (something similar) as well.

I would love to talk with them about what we offer and discuss how they could benefit also.

I have enclosed a stamped, addressed postcard for you to jot down the names and contact information for a couple of people that you think I should talk with about what we offer. If you prefer, you can email it to me at <email address>.

Thanks for your help.

If there's anything I can do for you, please let me know. [If they haven't received the item they purchased from you, comment about the anticipated delivery or completion date.]

Handwritten Notecard
To A New Purchaser

Instead of mailing something "typed," you may want to use something much less formal such as a handwritten notecard imprinted with your company name or logo and basic contact information on it to thank a new purchaser for doing business with you and to ask for a referral.

———

<First name or names of your new purchaser>,

Thank you for your placing your trust (confidence) in us for your <name or description of product or service>.

I have enjoyed getting to know you, and I could use your help in identifying some of your friends that you think should know about us.

I have enclosed a stamped, addressed postcard so you can let me know about anyone that you think should experience what we offer. If you prefer, you can email the information to me at <email address>.

Thanks for your help. If there's anything I can do for you, please let me know.

Email To A New Purchaser

Email is a convenient way to reach out to a new purchaser to thank them for doing business with you and to ask for a referral. Primarily you are requesting a referral since you're already sent them other notes and letters.

———

<First name of your new purchaser>,

Again, thank you for selecting (choosing) <name of company> (us) and letting (allowing) us serve you.

As you are enjoying (getting ready to start using, waiting on delivery/installation/completion of) your new <name or description of product or service>, I imagine that you probably have thought of several friends, associates, family members, and co-workers who might like to have one (something similar) as well.

I would love to talk with them about what we offer and discuss how we could help them also.

Just hit the "reply" button above and send me the names and contact information for a couple of people that you think need to hear what we're all about.

Thanks for your help. If there's anything I can do for you, please let me know.

Letter To An Established Customer

Use this typed or computer printed letter to contact someone who has been using your product or service for at least 6 months that you are sure is satisfied with you and your company. Your letter should again thank them for doing business with your company and then request their help in identifying people who should know about what you offer.

———

<First name or names of your customer or client>,

We (I) really enjoy having you (you and your family) (you and your company) as one of our satisfied customers (clients) and appreciate the confidence you have shown in me (our company, me and our company).

I could use your help.

I would love to be able to talk with some of your friends (colleagues, associates, relatives, co-workers, neighbors) that you think should know about <name or description of the product or service they are using that they obtained from you>.

Please use the enclosed stamped, addressed postcard to jot down the names and contact information for anyone that you think I should talk with about what we offer. If you prefer, you can use email.

I'll let you know what I find out after I speak with them.

Thanks again for your help. Let me know if I can do anything for you.

Printed Notecard To An Established Customer

Rather than a letter, you may choose to use a notecard imprinted with the name and logo of your company that you print out on your computer to contact an existing customer or client that has been using your product or service for at least 6 months that you are sure is satisfied with you and your company. It's less formal than a letter, and it is nice way to ask for referrals.

———

<First name or names of your customer or client>,

We (I) really appreciate having you (you and your family, you and your company) as one of our satisfied customers (clients).

I could use your help.

I would love to be able to talk with some of your friends or associates (colleagues, relatives, neighbors) that might like to know about what we provide so I can discuss how they could benefit from what we offer.

I have enclosed a stamped, addressed postcard for you to jot down the names and contact information for anyone that you think should hear or see what we're all about. If you prefer, you can email the information to me at <email address>.

I'll let you know what I find out when I speak with them.

Thanks again for your help. Let me know if I can do anything for you.

Handwritten Notecard To An Established Customer

Instead of mailing something "typed," you may want to use an informal handwritten notecard or commercial greeting card to reach out to your existing or established customers and clients and ask them for referrals.

––––––

<First name or names of your customer or client>,

I (We) really appreciate having you (you and your family, you and your company) as one of our satisfied customers (clients), and I could use your help.

I have enclosed a stamped, addressed postcard for you to jot down the names and contact information for anyone that you think should see what we're all about.

If you prefer, you can email the information to me at <email address> or drop it by the office.

Thanks again for your help. Let me know if I can do anything for you.

Email To An Established Customer

Use this less formal email message for a more immediate way to reach out to your established customers and clients and ask them for referrals.

<First name of your customer or client>,

I (We) really appreciate having you (you and your family, you and your company) as one of our satisfied customers (clients).

I could use your help.

I would love to be able to talk with (meet) some of your friends (colleagues, neighbors, relatives, associates) that you think might like to learn more about what I (we) offer and how I (we) can help them also.

Just hit the "reply" button and send along (include, furnish) their names and their contact information for anyone that you think needs to (should) hear (see) what we're all about.

I'll let you know what I find out after I speak with them.

Thanks again for your help. Let me know if I can do anything for you.

Letter To A "Lost Sale"

Use this typed or computer printed letter to contact someone you met with about your product or service that purchased it from someone else. Your letter should be cordial and professional. No sales message (it will be implied). Just request their help in identifying people who should know about what you offer. Be sure to use or add your name to the return address on the envelope.

———

<First name or names of your "lost" customer>,

I'm glad I got the opportunity to meet and work with you as you were looking for your new <name or description of product or service you showed them>. Thank you for considering <name of your company> (us).

My company and I congratulate you and wish you all the best with your decision.

However, I could use your help.

Even though you ultimately decided that our solution was not in line with what you needed right now, I would love to be able to talk with some of your friends (colleagues, associates, co-workers, relatives, neighbors) that you think should know about <name or description of the product or service you discussed with them>.

Please use the enclosed stamped, addressed postcard to jot down the names and contact information for anyone that you think I should talk with about what we offer. If you prefer, you can use email.

Thanks again for your help. Let me know if I can do anything for you.

Printed Notecard To A "Lost Sale"

This is one case where a letter may not be the best choice because it may appear too formal or not get opened. A notecard imprinted with the name and logo of your company that you print out on your computer to contact people who have purchased what you offer from someone else. This is a good format to use to congratulate them and ask for referrals.

––––––

<First name or names of your "lost" customer>,

I'm glad I got the opportunity to meet and work with you as you were looking for your new <name or

description of product or service you showed them>. Thank you for considering <name of your company> (us).

My company and I congratulate you and wish you all the best with your decision.

If there's anything I can do for you personally, please let me know.

If you know (can think of) anyone who might like to know more about what we offer, even though it turned out not to be for you, please let me know that also.

Again, best wishes for your success.

Handwritten Notecard To A "Lost Sale"

Instead of mailing something "typed," you may want to use something less formal such as a handwritten notecard to reach out to people who purchased from someone else to congratulate them and ask for referrals.

———

<First name or names of your "lost" customer>,

Thank you for considering <name of your company> (us).

My company and I congratulate you and wish you all the best with your decision.

If there's anything I can do for you personally, please let me know.

If you think of anyone who might like to know about what we are offering, please let me know that also.

Handwritten Greeting Card Note To A "Lost Sale"

Use this handwritten note on the inside of a purchased "Congratulations" greeting card as an enclosure to send to people who purchased from someone else as you congratulate them and ask for referrals.

<First name or names of your "lost" customer>,

My company and I congratulate you and wish you all the best with your decision.

If there's anything I can do for you personally, please let me know.

Also, if you think of anyone who might like what we offer, please let me know that also.

Email To A "Lost Sale"

Use this informal email message for a more immediate way to contact people who purchased from someone else as you congratulate them and ask for referrals. Don't use any attachments or graphics.

———

<First name of your former customer>,

I'm glad I got the opportunity to meet and work with you as you were looking for your new <name or description of product or service you showed them>.

Thank you for considering <name of your company> (us, me).

My company and I (We, All of us here at <name of your company>) congratulate you and wish you all the best with your decision.

If there's anything I can do for you personally, please let me know.

If you know or hear of anyone who might like to know about what we are offering, please let me know that also.

Again, best wishes for your continued success.

7

Making It Work

An Entrepreneurial Approach

As a salesperson responsible for your own production and income, you are an entrepreneur. No customers are provided or guaranteed, although some will respond to your marketing and contact you or arrive on their own.

Customers don't come in a box that you can purchase at the office supply store — it would be great if it was just that easy to create them.

Each day, you essentially start from scratch. You don't know how many you'll have a chance to talk with or who they will be. Some days there might not be anyone who walks through your front door or otherwise contacts you.

You examine your options for customers — the lifeblood of your business — and determine that you have *three* viable choices.

Your Three Customer Options

Option one — you stay in your sales center or showroom and greet the traffic that walks in, telephones, or emails from traditional marketing sources — principally supplied by your company.

This includes all forms of print advertising in newspapers and magazines (including specialty and consumer publications), electronic media (such as radio and TV), internet (your website, social media, and internet advertising), and broker or agent traffic.

Add to that any advertising you do on your own, including direct mail, email campaigns, or flyers.

Of course, you maintain post-visit Follow-Through® contact with everyone you meet according to their level of interest and ability to make a decision.

Option two — you reach out to people you don't know or haven't met. You involve strangers in your business and begin building sales and referrals with their help. This is discussed in my companion book for lead generation: "**Filling Your Funnel:** *Building Your Business By Reaching Out To Strangers.*"

Option three — you talk to people you already know

and begin developing your own leads with them. That is what we have been discussing in this book.

It's these second and third options that are going to give you the additional edge and earning power over other salespeople in your market.

Most salespeople are content to work with the traffic that directly contacts them, walks through their front door, or results from incidental referrals.

This is unpredictable and short-sided. It is not a dependable or consistent form of lead generation.

Empowering Yourself For Success

With the knowledge that you can produce your own leads and make traffic appear that you have generated, you can be an outstanding success.

This is powerful.

Some leads you will generate from people that you haven't met yet. You'll focus on making new connections with strangers and learning which ones you might be able to help and which can lead you to their friends.

However, starting with your circle of contacts and beginning there is very empowering. There is no pressure to meet people before you can start asking for help. Begin with people that you think might have a need for what you offer themselves or can lead you to others.

As long as you don't give the impression that your friendship is conditioned upon them buying from you or giving you the name of someone to talk with, your friendship will not be in jeopardy whether they can help you or not.

Knowledge is power, and in this case it is knowing that you can produce the sales leads you need to be successful. This is in addition to, or in place of, what you get through conventional marketing and advertising.

Begin acting as if the only traffic or sales leads you're going to get is what you produce for yourself. Then anything your company or marketing supplies is a bonus.

Empowerment Is Taken

By generating your own leads — by reaching out to people that you don't know in addition to utilizing your circle of contacts — you're going to be adding an element to your sales program that most sales organizations and salespeople are missing.

There is no effective limit to the number of leads that you can generate this way.

This truly can make the difference in your success and enable you to thrive in your marketplace when other companies and salespeople are just competing for the same pool of people.

Empowering yourself to begin generating your own leads — by working with either friends or strangers, or both — is not something you have to be invited to do or given permission to start.

Empowerment is taken. It is not given.

Just decide that generating your own leads is something that makes sense for you to do — even if you're not totally comfortable with the idea of approaching your family, friends, and acquaintances and talking with them about your business.

However, just doing that will empower you to begin expanding your business and taking responsibility for producing the most crucial element of your sales program — your future customers.

Going Beyond The Obvious

While talking to people that you already know and asking them for business or for referrals will net you many additional opportunities to make sales, other aggressive salespeople in your marketplace can do the same thing.

They may not be as comprehensive as you are or able to identify the variety of people you can contact, but starting with referrals from existing satisfied customers and from family and friends are common ways to generate more traffic.

Add to that, the professional network groups and associations that many salespeople share and try to use to attract sales, and you'll soon see that this is quite competitive.

However, when you begin to contact more than just your friends and associates that you know — more than just the obvious — you'll be doing what hardly anyone else in your market is doing.

When you reach out to people that you know from using their services or shopping at their stores, and even from "lost sales" (people who purchased from someone else), you're going to be finding opportunities that just aren't there for the people who aren't looking for them.

Then, you can also use some of the scenarios that are in my companion lead generation book, "**Filling Your Funnel:** *Building Your Business By Reaching Out To Strangers*," for meeting and working with strangers.

Reaching out to total strangers and strategically contacting other businesspeople and professionals in your marketplace that can help you in your business are ways that you can be intentional about expanding your business.

Few other sales organizations and salespeople in your market will come close to the type of lead generation you'll be capable of producing.

Intentionally Going After Success

Making the decision that you want to have more traffic than you're getting now through traditional sources — and that you want it on a more consistent basis — is the first step to becoming a great traffic generator.

It is a conscious decision, and it requires willpower. No one reaches this intentional decision without the earnest desire to act on it — unless it is just wishful thinking.

Wanting more traffic — such as wishing it would just show up — is entirely different than doing something to actually make it happen.

This works in all market conditions — very competitive markets to very stubborn ones.

As long as you have something to sell at a good value — and people to buy it, the techniques and strategies of traffic generation that I've discussed in this book will work for you.

You're In Charge Now

The amount of traffic you can produce is limited only by your ambition and the amount of time devoted to it.

You have been given several scenarios in this book. Expand from there. This is a good start, but it is not intended as a comprehensive list.

You have to own your customer base — not in a legal sense but in a responsibility one. You have to continually add to it so it doesn't get stale. Own the creation of additional leads.

Your paradigm needs to be that you're in charge of producing the people that you meet with in your sales center, showroom, or their location.

Act as if the only traffic you're going to get is what you produce for yourself.

Then anything else that comes your way through traditional marketing or incidental referrals is a bonus.

Not every person you talk to will want to or be able to help you, but as long as you are committed to developing your own leads, you are going to be successful.

You hold the key.

Steve Hoffacker

Steve Hoffacker, AICP, CAASH, CAPS, CGA, CGP, CMP, CSP, MCSP, MIRM, is principal of Hoffacker Associates LLC, a West Palm Beach, Florida based real estate and small business sales and marketing consultancy and commercial real estate brokerage.

Steve is an award-winning sales trainer and coach, marketing consultant, photographer, commercial real estate broker, blogger, teacher, best-selling author, writer, salesman, mentor, and motivational speaker.

For 30 years, he has helped homebuilders, salespeople (B2B and B2C), contractors, Realtors®, business owners, and entrepreneurs to be more visible, competitive, profitable, and effective — and to really enjoy what they are doing.

One of the keys to increased production and profitability is Steve's innovative customer connection program of intentional lead generation, customer rating, social networking, and post-visit contact that lets you reach out to potential customers, attract new leads, identify those people who are ready to make a decision, and maintain appropriate contact with others who need more time.

As a result, you will be making sales that otherwise might not have happened, and you can eliminate unnecessary expenditures of time, money, and energy in the process.

www.ingramcontent.com/pod-product-compliance
Lightning Source LLC
Chambersburg PA
CBHW060552210326
41519CB00014B/3447